W9-AVA-279

Fragile States

Fragile States

Violence and the Failure of Intervention

LOTHAR BROCK, HANS-HENRIK
HOLM, GEORG SØRENSEN AND
MICHAEL STOHL

polity

Copyright © Lothar Brock, Hans-Henrik Holm, Georg Sørensen and Michael Stohl 2012

The right of Lothar Brock, Hans-Henrik Holm, Georg Sørensen and Michael Stohl to be identified as Authors of this Work has been asserted in accordance with the UK Copyright, Designs and Patents Act 1988.

First published in 2012 by Polity Press
Reprinted 2012, 2013, 2014

Polity Press
65 Bridge Street
Cambridge CB2 1UR, UK

Polity Press
350 Main Street
Malden, MA 02148, USA

All rights reserved. Except for the quotation of short passages for the purpose of criticism and review, no part of this publication may be reproduced, stored in a retrieval system, or transmitted, in any form or by any means, electronic, mechanical, photocopying, recording or otherwise, without the prior permission of the publisher.

ISBN-13: 978-0-7456-4941-2
ISBN-13: 978-0-7456-4942-9(pb)

A catalogue record for this book is available from the British Library.

Typeset in 10.25 on 13 pt FF Scala
by Servis Filmsetting Ltd, Stockport, Cheshire
Printed and bound in USA by Edwards Brothers, Inc.

The publisher has used its best endeavours to ensure that the URLs for external websites referred to in this book are correct and active at the time of going to press. However, the publisher has no responsibility for the websites and can make no guarantee that a site will remain live or that the content is or will remain appropriate.

Every effort has been made to trace all copyright holders, but if any have been inadvertently overlooked the publisher will be pleased to include any necessary credits in any subsequent reprint or edition.

For further information on Polity, visit our website: www.politybooks.com

For our grandchildren:
Kaja, Jovan,
Katarina, Luna, Jonatan, Mira, Karla, Bastian, Benjamin,
Jonas, Tobias,
Sophia, Jasper, Samuel and Nina

Contents

Acknowledgements

This book is a follow-up to a series of five workshops conducted at Purdue University in West Lafayette, Florence, Italy and the University of California Santa Barbara over a period of five years in which the participants submitted papers and then met for five days and discussed the problem of fragile states, political violence and the response of the international community.

As was their purpose, the workshops brought together a rather disparate group of scholars representing very different intellectual traditions and approaches. Most of the workshop participants participated in three or more of the five meetings. They included Chadwick F. Alger, Mohammed Ayoob, William Bain, Christopher Clapham, Robert Dorff, Peter Grabosky, Ted Robert Gurr, Robert Jackson, Jennifer Jackson-Preece, Leslie Janzen, George Lopez, Ann Mason, Steven Metz, Michael Nicholson, Alpa Patel, Scott Reid, Dan Smith, Hans-Joachim Spanger, Rachel Stohl and Peter Wallensteen.

Sponsorship for three of the meetings came from the Strategic Outreach Program of the US Army War College. We thank the Army War College for its financial assistance and all the participants in our workshops for their substantial contributions to our understanding of the issue.

We greatly appreciate the invitation from our editor Louise Knight and Polity Press to contribute to the series of which this book is a part and also thank the anonymous readers who took time to read the manuscript and to provide us with several constructive suggestions for improvement.

Introduction

War and Conflict in Today's World

Something has happened when it comes to war and conflict in today's world. It is not that violent conflict has disappeared; there is plenty of it, and some conflicts are even more destructive and devastating in terms of human cost than previously. But we commonly think about large-scale violent conflict – that is, war – as something that takes place between two or more countries. The very definition of war in *Webster's Dictionary* reflects this view; war is simply defined as 'a state of usually open and declared armed hostile conflict between states or nations'.

It is this kind of thinking about war which is increasingly obsolete. In the first half of the twentieth century, conflict escalated into two world wars. Since then, the number of interstate wars has been in decline. This trend has continued after the end of the Cold War. Since 1989, there have been a total of 128 armed conflicts – most of them minor, 48 of them wars (defined as armed conflict in which at least 1,000 people are killed, or killed yearly). Only eight of these conflicts were interstate; the rest of them were *intrastate* (Harbom and Wallensteen, 2009).

We have therefore experienced a fundamental shift in the nature of armed conflict, including war. Such conflict is now much more *intrastate* than it is *interstate*. However, in some cases these intrastate conflicts were internationalized in the sense that an external state or group of states intervened in the conflict, as in the Democratic Republic of the Congo, where several neighbouring states supported one side or the other. In the case of the Georgia war of 2008, a Russian force supported the Ossetians against Georgia. In 1999, NATO intervened in the Serbian war in Kosovo, and in 2011, it intervened in the uprising in Libya. Still, these conflicts are primarily intrastate, related to the peculiar characteristics of the countries affected by violence. These countries are widely defined as fragile states. State fragility is not automatically accompanied by a breakdown of order and collective violence. New research rather shows that the absence of a consolidated state may be compensated by various other ways of governance (Hagmann and Péclard, 2010: 542). Nevertheless, where there *is* large-scale, intrastate violence there tends to be state fragility. For that reason, it is necessary to engage in the analysis of fragile states in order to understand what it is that generates and shapes war and conflict today, the theme of the book series of which this volume is a part.

This book offers such an inquiry. In concrete terms, the book will clarify the concept of 'fragile state' and discuss it in relation to other popular concepts such as 'weak' and 'failed' states; explain how fragile states emerge in terms of pre-colonial, colonial and post-colonial history; set forth the core characteristics of fragile statehood as a Weberian ideal type, but also address the differences between countries owing to dissimilar trajectories; analyse the connection between fragile statehood and violent conflict with special reference to the Democratic Republic of the Congo, Afghanistan and Haiti; analyse the role of international society in relation to fragile statehood and explain – again with special reference to the three cases – why the role of outsiders in addressing the problems is necessarily limited; identify a few successes – that is, countries which 'ought to be' fragile, but which are not, owing to particular circumstances; and offer a (pessimistic) view of the future of most fragile states.

The Decreasing Importance of Interstate War

Some commentators believe that the decline in interstate wars will be reversed. They claim that 'the world has become normal again', in the sense that 'nations remain as strong as ever, and so too the nationalist ambitions, the passions, and the competition among nations that have shaped history' (Kagan, 2007: 1). From this view, the rise of non-democratic powers like China and Russia will pave the way for aggressive power balancing and potential violent conflict.

But there are strong arguments for diagnosing a more permanent transformation of interstate relations. First, there are a number of consolidated liberal democracies in the international system; they have created a very high level of economic, political and social integration among themselves. In the context of the EU, the development of supranational authority and free movement across borders set a new framework where countries may continue to be formally independent, but at the same time are deeply integrated in a cross-border community. In such a framework, the use of organized violence to solve conflicts is no longer an option; the countries which waged two world wars have within a few decades become a security community (Adler and Barnett, 1998; Deutsch et al., 1957).

The forces of political and economic integration are relevant elsewhere also, and that further reduces the risk of interstate war. The newly emerging powers – such as Brazil, China, India or South Africa – know that the road to success involves deep involvement in economic globalization; by no means does it call for territorial conquest. In this sense, these countries are following the 'trading state' path set by Japan and Germany after the Second World War (Rosecrance, 1986, 1999), even though they believe in having considerable military capabilities reinforcing their bid for voice on the global level. Secondly, new regional communities such as the African

Union (AU), the Union of South American States (UNASUR) and the Association of East Asian Nations (ASEAN) have the potential to develop into security communities, though they may differ from the Western type referred to above. Thirdly, there is some hope that the normative basis of global co-operation may be strengthened by further democratization, although 'the third wave' of democratization identified by Samuel Huntington in many instances got stuck and resulted in 'defect democracies'.

These changes have been accompanied by increasing respect for the 'territorial integrity norm' – that is, 'the pro-scription that force should not be used to alter interstate boundaries' (Zacher, 2001: 215). That norm emerged in the context of the League of Nations after the First World War. It was generally accepted as an element in the UN Charter in 1945 and it has been strengthened since the mid-1970s. Thus, from 1976 to the present, 'no major cases of successful terri-torial aggrandizement have occurred' (Zacher, 2001: 237). In short, classical war between states is either irrelevant (among consolidated liberal democracies) or in sharp decline (among emerging economies and other modernizing states). Our argument is not that interstate war will never take place again. In some regions, such as the Middle East or in Kashmir, there is a continuing risk of war between states. But large-scale vio-lent conflict is now overwhelmingly intrastate, taking place in fragile states, though, as stated above, not all fragile states are equally conflict prone and the frequency of intrastate conflict varies as well.

Fragile States: A Different Kind of Statehood

We may feel that we have always lived in a world of sover-eign states. However, the global system of sovereign states is actually quite recent and developed as a result of the process of decolonization following the Second World War. The system of states has been greatly expanded since then, with the number of member states of the United Nations growing from 5 at its founding in 1945 to its current membership of 192. Western-style modern states, with polities based on law, order and centralized rule, developed economies and defined nations (i.e. groups of people which make up a legal, cultural and emotional community), developed to full maturity only in the twentieth century and in non-linear ways (see the emergence of Fascism and Stalinism). Human history, then, is not a history of sovereign statehood; far from it. During most of human history most people have resided in communities with overlapping loyalties or empires with contested borders. These communities lacked the major features which are usually associated with contemporary sovereign states. The study of international relations has tended to underline the similarities of states; that is, to treat states as 'like units'. J. D. B. Miller expressed it in the following way: 'Just as we know a camel or a chair when we see one, so we know a sovereign state. It is a political entity which is treated as a sovereign state by other sovereign states' (Miller, 1981: 16). For many realist scholars of international relations, the sovereign state is a given point of departure and not a subject of investigation; focus is on the relations between states, not on their different qualities.

Economic liberals, in contrast, address the (internal) characteristics of states. But they, too, follow a uniform image of a functioning state in as much as they have tended to see weak and fragile statehood as a transitory stage of development which would be solved once Third World countries followed the same developmental path as taken earlier by the developed countries in the West: a progressive journey from a traditional, pre-industrial, agrarian, non-democratic society towards a modern, industrial, democratic mass-consumption society. But this evolutionary view is wrong; there is no in-built law of history ensuring that progress and modernity as we now understand them will emerge.

In terms of the long lines of history, the state as it currently exists is a relatively new arrival. That insight should prompt us to study historical trajectories of state formation in different parts of the world. When we do so, we recognize that the historical pathways to statehood are characterized by extreme variation: early state formation in China had little resemblance to later state formation in Russia; state formation in Western Europe was even different from that in the USA (Darwin, 2007). The larger point is that there is no linear process leading from the communities of hunters and gatherers to the modern nation-state. Rather, state formation proceeds in dissimilar ways and moves in different directions. The path taken to effective, democratic and economically robust statehood in Europe and North America has not been replicated in many parts of the world, even as all countries have adopted the formal characteristics of sovereign statehood and in this sense may be considered as part of a global culture of the nation-state (Meyer et al., 1997). In earlier days, many of the entities which we now characterize as fragile states were not sovereign members of the international system of states. Most often these entities were colonies or tributary entities, dependent on and dominated by the colonial motherland or hegemonic powers. Today, the sovereign state system is a global institution. The contemporary system contains a range and variety of states that are far more diverse not only in terms of their cultures, religions, languages and ideologies, but also in their forms of government, military capacity, levels of economic development, and so on, than ever before precisely because former dependencies are now part of the system.

Nonetheless, with all the heterogeneity in the world of states, there are some basic functions which all states are expected to fulfil in order to merit being called states. Among these are the provision of both security and material well-being. Failures to provide these two functions are not simply expressions of doing things differently but also evidence of doing them badly. In this sense, the terminology of failed, weak or fragile states is not only descriptive, but also has a normative connotation: states are not functioning as they should. This terminology is, of course, inspired by the Weberian ideal type of a modern bureaucratic state. Looking through these lenses may tempt us to ignore the variety of ways in which weak government may be compensated by strong societies (Migdal, 1998). Thus, speaking in terms of state failure, weakness or fragility may reflect more our image of a well-functioning state than the realities on the ground. However, if there is a persistent gap between the ideals to which the self-description of states refers, on the one hand, and the practice of governance, on the other, then there is good reason to address this gap and its domestic and international consequences. In this sense we use fragile statehood as a term which highlights the failures of governance in specific structural settings.

Fragile states, then, may not be on the path towards the Weberian model of a state. Rather, they may be dominated by social forces and political groups who use the language of modernity and development to legitimize the exploitation of the state as a source of private enrichment. This is one of the factors which abets violent conflict, though the causal relations between state fragility are quite complex, as we will discuss in chapter 3.

The Debate about Fragile States and the Contribution of This Book

The concept of 'fragile states' is a recent invention. From the 1960s and up to the end of the Cold War, politicians and scholars were concerned about 'developing countries', 'newly

independent nations' or 'post-colonial states'. The dominant view of these entities was informed by Western, liberal
modernization theory: it claimed that tradition would soon
make room for modernity and that the less developed countries, therefore, would follow in the footsteps of the Western
vanguard. This view was a result of the profound optimism
sparked by the rapid development of Britain in the nineteenth century and of the USA in the twentieth. John Stuart
Mill claimed that 'whoever knows the political economy of
England, or even Yorkshire, knows that of all nations, actual
or possible' (quoted from Kingston-Mann, 1999: 132). This
modernization view was propagated by many Western observers during the Cold War; it was a way of emphasizing the
developed countries of the West as the attractive and natural
model of development for latecomers.

Paradoxically, this optimistic view faded when Western
thought seemed triumphant. For a brief moment the end of
the Cold War sparked Western euphoria, animated by the
notion of the 'end of history'. With the breakdown of social-
ism, modernity and liberal democracy seemed to arrive
everywhere and much quicker than expected. But the mood
soon darkened owing to the lack of progress in many poor
countries combined with the persistence of old and the emergence of new violent conflict, now mostly within fragile states.
In the mid-1990s, the tyranny, lawlessness, crime, disease,
environmental stress and demographic pressures of West
Africa led Robert Kaplan to claim that major parts of the world
were descending into chaos. For that reason the most important feature of the new world (dis-)order in his view was one
of 'the coming anarchy' (Kaplan, 1994). Such fears escalated
after the terrorist attacks of September 11, 2001. Epitomizing
the new mood, the National Security Strategy of the United
States of 2002 stated that the country was now threatened
less by conquering states than by failing ones. The European

Union followed suit by claiming, in its 2003 Security Strategy, that state fragility constituted a major threat to European security.

Thus, failing, weak or fragile states, as they are mostly called today, have become a central issue not only of development cooperation but also of security politics in the West. However, though the concept is new, the problem behind it is not, and it is most likely to last. It is for this very reason that the issue has generated extensive academic work. Much of this work focuses on finding certain keys for explaining state fragility, like ethnic cleavages, patrimonialism or the resource curse. The present analysis focuses on combining the identification of common features of state fragility with addressing variation in state performance (di John, 2010: 24). We do so by looking specifically into the interaction between domestic and international factors. In pursuing this course, we will focus on the linkage between state fragility, collective violence and the use of force in dealing with fragile states.

We proceed on the assumption that the modernization view prevailing during the first two decades after decolonization was misleading because it misinterpreted both the past and the future. In the past, as we will discuss more fully in the next chapter, states around the world had experienced trajectories which are radically different from the typical path taken by the now developed West. The future, of course, is not predetermined. There is no guarantee, nor is it even very likely, that most fragile states will follow in the footsteps of the consolidated and successful ones. Just as their historical experiences are different from the successful states, their futures are most likely different as well, as we will discuss in chapter 2.

The earliest radical critique of modernization theory, developed in the late 1960s and onwards, came from neo-Marxist dependency theorists. They emphasized that peripheral states in the capitalist world system had been subjected to underdevelopment as a consequence of the process by which capitalist forces from the developed core countries expanded to subdue and impoverish the Third World. The argument proposed that earlier forms of society in the Third World may have been *un*developed, but *under*development began only with the arrival of global capitalism. That is, global capitalism in one single process generates development and wealth (in the industrialized world) and underdevelopment and poverty (in the Third World).

Radical dependency theory has a point: external domination is a major element in the formation of fragile states, as we argue in chapter 2. But dependency scholars also downplayed or ignored domestic factors in their analyses, such as the role of domestic elites. With independence, the latter became increasingly important for the political and social development of the respective countries. Thus, fragile states have emerged from a mixture of domestic and international conditions, both of which are fundamentally unlike anything experienced by the successful states in the West.

As pointed out above, state fragility became an issue with the outbreak (or persistence) of collective violence in some of the post-colonial states which went along with gross violations of human rights. This violence was mostly attributed to a vicious circle between deficient government, social cleavages and serious shortcomings in economic development. State and nation building, in combination with continued economic assistance and a call for more consistent humanitarian intervention, were the order of the day. Yet, not all states with limited territorial control and a weak economy experienced violence. Thus, there is need for a closer look at the linkage between fragile states and violent conflict. We deal with these issues in chapter 3.

September 11, 2001, set a different context for the debate about fragile states. The 9/11 attacks helped re-emphasize the

Bush administration's priority given to national security, but it also changed the attitude towards involvement in fragile states. The 2002 US National Security Strategy pledged to

> extend the benefits of freedom across the globe. We will actively work to bring the hope of democracy, free markets, and free trade to every corner of the world. The events of September 11, 2001, taught us that weak states, like Afghanistan, can pose as great a danger to our national interests as strong states. Poverty does not make poor people into terrorists and murderers. Yet poverty, weak institutions, and corruption can make weak states vulnerable to terrorist networks and drug cartels within their borders. (NSS, 2002: 2)

In other words, the humanitarian impulse towards intervention was supplemented by a national security impulse. Some commentators hoped that this would 'stiffen humanitarianism with the iron fist of national security' (Farer, 2003: 88–9). But national security concerns and humanitarian concerns do not always overlap; the security factor has not helped amplify the humanitarian factor (Jentleson, 2007: 284). Humanitarian concerns are still in play, but only 'selectively on the basis of "national interests" of the interveners' (Bellamy, 2004: 145). In sum, the policy of active intervention in fragile states has been much strengthened compared to the Cold War days in the sense that humanitarian and/or security concerns may lead to intervention, including intervention by force, in such states (Geis et al., 2006). But intervention remains highly selective, undertaken in some cases but not in other cases, even if humanitarian (e.g. Sudan, Myanmar) and/ or security (e.g. Iran, Pakistan) concerns would seem to point in that direction.

When intervention is eventually undertaken by the use of significant force in the contemporary era, the purpose is not an old-fashioned conquest. The purpose is rather to replace a weak state by a strong state in the sense of promoting state building, democratization and economic development. This, then, is the current major issue on the analytical agenda concerning fragile states: to what extent is it at all possible for outsiders to meet the ambition of creating effective and responsive states that can spearhead a process of democratization and socio-economic development? On one side in this debate are profound optimists who find that good planning and sufficient resources can lead to 'fixing failed states' (Ghani and Lockhart, 2008). On the other side are similarly profound pessimists who argue that such projects face insurmountable obstacles, even to the extent that external intervention can have the opposite effect, namely state decline and disintegration (Chandler, 2006).

As we will argue in chapter 4, we are among the pessimists. The position of outsiders coming into fragile states with ambitious projects is tenuous at best. They are going home sooner rather than later, and any long-term sustainable improvements depend on the active and constructive involvement of insiders. But in a large number of cases, there is insufficient demand among local elites for the creation of effective and responsive states. They rather have other projects in mind which perpetuate their control and access to resources. Some elements of state building may be the outcome of outside involvement, but as a matter of rule they fall short of creating markedly stronger states. We explain this in detail in chapter 4. At the same time, there is an intervention fatigue, because of the failures and troubles of both security-motivated (e.g. Afghanistan, Iraq) and humanitarian interventions. In the immediate future international society will probably be less rather than more active when it comes to facing the problems in fragile states.

Our case studies focus on Afghanistan, Haiti and the Congo. We emphasize that they are fragile states with particularly grave problems. This surely helps underline our pessimistic analysis. There are better possibilities for many other fragile states where there is a mixture of constructive and destructive elements. Some states that appeared set up for failure instead developed rather efficient government, capable economies and strong national communities. In order to explain this, we focus on the trajectories of Botswana and Costa Rica in chapter 5. This will help clarify the factors that led away from fragility and towards stronger statehood.

In sum, we have briefly outlined the debates about what are now called fragile states as they have developed over the last several decades. In so doing, we have situated the contribution of this work in the context of these debates. The next chapter identifies major characteristics of fragile states. Chapter 2 discusses the formation of fragile states and lays out the special pathway to fragile statehood. Chapter 3 explores the linkage between fragile states and conflict in detail. Chapter 4 is focused on the role of outsiders and explains how both domestic and international conditions impede successful interventions in fragile states. Chapter 5 analyses how fragility was escaped in the cases of Costa Rica and Botswana. Chapter 6 sums up our analysis and discusses the implications for analysts and policy makers.

CHAPTER ONE

Major Characteristics of Fragile States

As stated above, the world of states is full of diversity, and so naturally it follows that this is also the case when it comes to fragile states. It is true that every single state is unique in terms of historical development and precise characteristics. Against this background, some observers are critical of any overall concept of fragile or failed state. Their claim is that conceptual stretching is taken too far; these general labels include cases that are enormously diverse. For example, Somalia was a collapsed state for almost a decade in the sense that the state apparatus ceased to exist; but Sudan, Iraq and North Korea are not collapsed states, even if they are considered fragile. Some states are weak in terms of formal institutional capacity (e.g. Chad), but Colombia is not a weak state in this sense, though it certainly is with regard to its ability to control domestic conflict. Some states, such as Liberia and Sierra Leone, are war-torn for long periods, but fragile states such as Bangladesh and North Korea are not at war (examples from Call, 2008).

All this is true, but the insight that every state is unique does not preclude their having common characteristics which allow us to pool them in a group. Surrendering to arguments of historical specificity will not permit us to address the principal ways in which fragile statehood differs from successful modern statehood. In this latter category, there are also vastly different entities: consider Canada, Iceland, France, the Netherlands, Spain and Denmark. In order to discover principal differences, we need summarizing concepts. Such concepts should always be followed by empirical differentiation and concrete nuances, but the necessity of the latter is no argument for giving up on the former. Without more general concepts, any overall consideration about what is going on in the world of states will have a hard time indeed. Giving up on summarizing concepts is the first step towards giving up on theory altogether.

If one accepts the need for such concepts, the next question is whether 'fragile states' is the best label for the problem we want to talk about. We are inspired by the fact that many international organizations and observers now use that term (Engberg-Petersen et al., 2008). Competing terms suffer from various drawbacks. The notion of 'failed' or 'failing' state indicates the emergence of an acute problem that can be quickly remedied, but fragile states have a long history and in most cases quick remedy is not possible. Failure should sooner be seen as an aggravation of the governance problems pertaining to fragile states. 'Quasi-states' was suggested by Robert Jackson (1990). He connects the term closely to the special process of decolonization after the Second World War, but fragile states can also emerge in the absence of colonization and decolonization, as we will see in the next chapter. Finally, 'weak states' has been a much-used term; but since 'strong states' are often thought of as militarily strong entities and/or authoritarian states, 'weak' may send the wrong message. Yet the question of labelling is not crucial here; as long as we accept that summarizing concepts are needed, who wins the terminological beauty contest is less important.

The summarizing concept of 'fragile state' is best formulated as a Weberian ideal type. The ideal type is an attempt to capture core characteristics of a given phenomenon in its pure form. In so doing it focuses on what is more important and disregards what is less important. Marx's analysis of capitalism, for example, constructs an ideal type of the capitalist mode of production. The empirical basis is capitalism in England, but the concept centres on what Marx sees as the most important characteristics of capitalism rather than on a summary of concrete English reality. Weber's concept of 'Protestant Ethic' is another example of an ideal type.

In our case, we are looking for the core characteristics of fragile statehood. Let us begin with the state in the narrow sense: the government and the state apparatus. Institutional and administrative structures in fragile states are inefficient and corrupt. Rule is based on selective coercion rather than legitimacy and the rule of law. There are no effective mechanisms for holding leaders accountable to the populations. Weber famously defined the state as 'a human community that [successfully] claims the *monopoly of the legitimate use of physical force* within a given territory' (Weber, 1946: 78). In this regard, the essence of statehood is enforcement: the capacity to make people comply with the state's laws (Fukuyama, 2004: 21). But note that, according to Weber, enforcement cannot be based only on coercion understood as the state's power over society; it is also based on legitimacy: that is, power through society. Michael Mann (1984) calls this infrastructural power; it entails a cooperative relationship between citizens and their government (Migdal, 2001).

So, fragile states are ineffective in terms of ability to plan and execute state-defined policies and they lack legitimacy in terms of being considered lawful and just by the population. But fragile states are also characterized by particular conditions in society. The economy is the material or physical basis of the state. Fragile states lack coherent national economies which are capable of sustaining a basic level of welfare for the population and of providing resources for running an effective state. Defective economies often depend crucially on the world market because they are mono-economies based on the export of one or a few primary goods. The economy is often highly heterogeneous, containing not only elements of a modern sector but also pre-capitalist structures in agriculture. In both urban and rural sectors, large parts of the population are outside of the formal economic sector, living in localized subsistence economies at very low standards.

Finally, there is a more abstract but no less important aspect: the idea of the state itself (Buzan, 1991: 69). This concerns the extent to which the people within the physical state's territory make up a community. There are two major facets of community. One concerns citizenship, meaning relations between citizens and the state. In well-functioning countries, the state provides political, legal and socio-economic rights for citizens, who in return have a number of obligations, such as paying taxes. The other facet can be called 'community of sentiment'. It concerns the extent to which citizens consider themselves part of a community with a common language and common cultural and historical identities. Benedict Anderson (1991) refers to communities of sentiment as 'imagined communities'.

In fragile states, the sovereign state's physical boundaries do not correspond to the boundaries of the imagined communities with which the people who reside within them most identify. In these states, ethnic identities connected to tribal, religious and similar characteristics continue to dominate over the national identity. The national community of sentiment has not grown strong, partly because the state has not been able to create effective citizenship. The substance of citizenship – legal, political and social rights – has not been provided. When the state does not deliver, people turn elsewhere for the satisfaction of material and non-material needs, predominantly towards ethnic communities. Loyalties are then projected in that direction and ethnic identities are reinforced. In sum, fragile states are characterized by a situation where neither the 'community of citizens', nor the 'community of sentiment' has developed to become the primary bond for people at the national level.

Table 1.1 summarizes the major characteristics of fragile states.

Many definitions of fragile statehood share our focus on the state's ineffectiveness and illegitimacy (e.g. Goldstone, 2009: 5). But then they also move in other directions. A brief comparison with the definition offered by the Development Assistance Committee (DAC) of the Organization for Economic Co-operation and Development (OECD) may help clarify the choices we have made. DAC suggests the following definition: 'States are fragile when state structures lack political will and/or capacity to provide the basic functions needed for poverty reduction, development, and to safeguard the security and human rights of their populations' (OECD, 2007).

First, the OECD definition helpfully underlines that state fragility is a matter of both structures and actors. Actors

Table 1.1. The fragile state	
Government	Inefficient and corrupt administrative and institutional structures. Rule based on selective coercion rather than on the rule of law. Monopoly on the legitimate use of violence not established. Low level of state legitimacy.
Economy	Lack of coherent national economies, capable of sustaining a basic level of welfare for the population and of providing resources for running an effective state. Amalgamations of traditional agriculture, an informal, petty urban sector and some fragments of modern industry. Significant dependence on the world market and on external economic interests.
Nationhood	Citizenship rights not provided; a divided population with predominance of local/ethnic community. Neither the 'community of citizens' nor the 'community of sentiment' has developed to become the primary bond among people at the national level.

within fragile states may be willing to do good things (e.g. Julius Nyerere when he was head of state in Tanzania), but they can be impeded by structures or by other actors. Both structures and actors must therefore be part of the analysis; in our ideal-type definition, the problem with fragility concerns both structures and actors, so we don't need the 'and/or' element. Second, the definition is focused on the state in the narrow sense of the government and the state apparatus. We argue that fragile statehood also concerns conditions in the surrounding society, especially as regards the situation of the economy and of the relationship between people. This helps emphasize that a movement towards less fragile statehood concerns not merely the state in the narrow sense, but also basic conditions in society. Third, the definition indicates that the problems with fragile states are of national origin, situated within the borders of the state. But we argue that international actors also bear responsibility for the emergence and persistence of fragile states and that element needs to enter the analysis. Fourth, the DAC definition tends to ask too much of fragile states; they are required to provide development, security, poverty reduction and human rights. This is a big menu. It can be argued that even several of the advanced, consolidated democracies in the Western world are unable to provide all this. Very poor states are often unable to supply all the material needs of their population even if they are highly disposed to do so.

Fifth, and most importantly, the DAC definition is ensnared by modernization thinking in its indication that all fragile states can get their act together and shed fragility by quickly becoming effective states that will provide for the good life for their citizens. This view of fragile states is further enhanced by developments in, and the aspirations of, international society. The Millennium Declaration (UN, 2000), adopted by 189 states at the UN General Assembly in 2000, makes a commitment towards realizing 'the good life' for every human being on the planet. It promises to promote peace, security, development, human rights and environmental protection for all. These are respectable and desirable goals, of course, but as we have indicated, many fragile states will not be able to meet them. They are, for reasons we will explain below, more likely to be caught in a situation of 'blocked development'.

Some critics argue that the notion of fragile or failed states amounts to 'an ideology of the imperialism of our time' (Jones, 2005). The charges are several: first, the term is purely descriptive, modelled on an ahistorical and ideal notion of what the 'perfect' state should look like and, therefore, it does not explain the historical emergence of fragile states. Second, 'the defining flaw' according to this critique is that state fragility is being identified as primarily '*local, indigenous*' in origin. In effect, the 'historically specific, international and local social relations' that have given rise to states caught in social, political and economic crisis are not identified (quotes from Jones, 2005: 4–6).

We find this particular critique misleading. The term is not purely descriptive, provided it is followed by an identification of the core characteristics of fragile statehood. Furthermore, this need not lead to ahistorical analysis. The next chapter is devoted to analysing different historical pathways to fragile statehood. We wholeheartedly agree that indexes of fragile states cannot stand alone; they need to be accompanied by concrete analysis of specific cases. The analysis will make clear that there are both international and domestic causes of, and pathways to, fragile statehood. In sum, we find the concept useful and the potentially 'imperialist' overtones avoidable. This approach does not preclude a closer look at non-Weberian types of governance which until now may have escaped the attention of those involved in the analysis of fragile statehood (Hagman and Péclard, 2010).

Which Are the Fragile States?

We have identified the core features of fragile statehood. Given this background, which are the fragile states? Answering that question requires additional conceptual work and a substantial amount of measurement. The general characteristics set forth above need to be connected to operational indicators which are then used to estimate the fragility of individual countries. It is fortunate that there are a number of existing 'conceptualizers' and 'quantifiers' of fragile states (for an instructive overview of these, see Rice and Stewart, 2008: 5–8).

We choose to employ the Failed States Index provided by the Fund for Peace and *Foreign Policy*. The index relies on three baskets of indicators: social, economic and political. Each of these can be used as proxy for the major features of fragile states according to our definition: *social* indicators measure aspects of what we call nationhood; *economic* indicators measure the status of the economy; and *political* indicators measure major dimensions of what we call government. Table 1.2 details the elements for each indicator.

We are aware that these indicators may not be perfect operational measures of a fragile state, but they are sufficient for our present purpose. Remember that any index must be considered a first overview of, or approximation to, the subject. An index tends to convey objectivity where there are a lot of discretionary choices involved. Still, it gives some clues as to what may be important and to what extent the identified factors correlate. In any case a detailed analysis of specific cases is necessary in order to ascertain in a more precise and profound manner the concrete characteristics of fragility in single states. First, however, we present the index of the twenty most fragile states in the world in 2011 in descending order (Table 1.3).

Twelve different indicators were used to estimate the three

Table 1.2 Indicators of fragile statehood
Social indicators
I-1 Mounting demographic pressures
I-2 Massive movement of refugees or internally displaced persons creating complex humanitarian emergencies
I-3 Legacy of vengeance-seeking group grievance or group paranoia
I-4 Chronic and sustained human flight
Economic indicators
I-5 Uneven economic development along group lines
I-6 Sharp and/or severe economic decline
Political indicators
I-7 Criminalization and/or delegitimization of the state
I-8 Progressive deterioration of public services
I-9 Suspension or arbitrary application of the rule of law and widespread violation of human rights
I-10 Security apparatus operates as a 'state within a state'
I-11 Rise of factionalized elites
I-12 Intervention of other states or external political actors

Source: Fund for Peace, *www.fundforpeace.org/global/?q=indicators* (accessed 8 July 2011).

aspects of fragile statehood. Each indicator is rated on a 1 to 10 scale with 1 (low) being the most stable and 10 (high) being the most unstable and in danger of collapse. Sweden, for example, provides public services to a very high degree; that produces a score of 1 or 2 on indicator 8, while Somalia's inability to provide almost any public services would call for a score of 10. Aggregated data are then normalized and scaled from 0 to 10 in order to obtain final scores for the twelve indicators covering 177 countries. As indicated above, the ideal-type approach to the definition of fragile states singles out the characteristics of fragile states in their pure – that is to say, most extreme – form. Those extreme characteristics are not equally true of all the states we shall consider fragile. There are different degrees of weakness, which means that there is great variation both in the aggregated 'averages' of the various fragile states, and with regard to which of the compo-

Table 1.3. Index of fragile states, 2011

Rank	Country	1-1	1-2	1-3	1-4	1-5	1-6	1-7	1-8	1-9	1-10	1-11	1-12	Total
1	Somalia	9.7	10.0	9.5	8.2	8.4	9.3	9.8	9.4	9.7	10.0	9.8	9.7	113.4
2	Chad	9.2	9.5	9.4	8.0	8.9	8.5	9.8	9.6	9.3	9.2	9.8	9.1	110.3
3	Sudan	8.5	9.6	9.9	8.2	9.1	6.4	9.4	9.0	9.7	9.6	9.9	9.5	108.7
4	Dem. Rep. of Congo	9.7	9.6	8.3	7.7	9.2	8.7	9.0	8.9	9.2	9.6	8.8	9.5	108.2
5	Haiti	10.0	9.2	7.3	8.9	8.8	9.2	9.4	10.0	8.0	8.4	8.8	10.0	108.0
6	Zimbabwe	9.3	8.2	9.0	9.3	9.2	9.0	9.3	9.0	9.2	9.0	9.6	7.8	107.9
7	Afghanistan	9.1	9.3	9.3	7.2	8.4	8.0	9.7	8.5	8.8	9.8	9.4	10.0	107.5
8	Central African Republic	8.9	9.6	8.6	5.8	8.9	8.1	9.1	9.0	8.6	9.7	9.1	9.6	105.0
9	Iraq	8.3	9.0	9.0	8.9	9.0	7.0	8.7	8.0	8.6	9.5	9.6	9.3	104.8
10	Ivory Coast	8.1	8.5	8.7	7.9	8.0	7.7	9.5	8.4	8.6	8.6	9.1	9.7	102.8
11	Guinea	8.2	7.7	7.9	8.3	8.4	8.6	9.4	8.7	9.2	9.3	9.2	7.6	102.5
12	Pakistan	8.8	9.2	9.3	7.5	8.5	6.6	8.6	7.3	8.7	9.4	9.1	9.3	102.3
13	Yemen	8.7	8.4	8.6	6.9	8.3	7.7	8.6	8.7	7.7	9.3	9.3	8.2	100.3
14	Nigeria	8.3	6.0	9.6	7.7	9.0	7.3	9.0	9.0	8.6	9.1	9.5	6.9	99.9
15	Niger	9.8	6.6	7.8	6.2	7.9	8.9	8.9	9.5	8.2	8.0	8.6	8.7	99.1
16	Kenya	8.8	8.5	8.7	7.6	8.5	7.0	8.9	7.8	7.7	7.9	8.8	8.5	98.7
17	Burundi	9.1	8.7	8.2	6.2	8.1	8.5	8.2	8.8	8.0	7.7	8.2	9.0	98.6
18	Myanmar	8.2	8.0	8.7	6.0	9.0	7.9	9.7	8.3	9.0	8.5	8.3	6.7	98.3
19	Guinea Bissau	8.7	7.2	5.4	7.4	8.1	8.7	9.2	8.4	7.8	9.3	9.2	8.8	98.3
20	Ethiopia	9.1	8.2	8.4	7.2	8.2	7.7	7.5	8.4	8.5	7.9	9.0	8.1	98.2

Source: The Fund for Peace, *www.fundforpeace.org/global/?q=fsi-grid2011* (accessed 11 July 2011)

nent dimensions within individual states are weakest (social, economic or political dimensions of state fragility). It should also be made clear that many states beyond the top twenty share many of these weaknesses, so this is an arbitrary cut-off point. Furthermore, it is also important to stress that many local areas within otherwise more or less stable states such as Colombia or the Philippines have the characteristics of fragile states. At the same time, there is considerable agreement among the leading indexes on which are the *most* fragile states overall.

A first measure of differentiation between types of fragile states emerges from the dissimilar scores in each of the twelve baskets; even among the most fragile states scores vary significantly between the three sets of indicators. But this is not enough: the different pathways to fragile statehood and the concrete make-up of individual states need to be considered as well. To repeat: the label of fragile state is a first approximation that must always be accompanied by concrete analysis of single cases. This is the subject of the next chapter.

CHAPTER TWO

The Formation of Fragile States

The comparative history of state formation is a huge subject because it must cover every major civilization in the world across several millennia; therefore, it is far from fully explored. Most studies have focused on the emergence of effective and legitimate states in Europe, but even here much remains to be examined. Accordingly the following considerations must be considered as a brief report from a work in progress where scholars continue to identify new elements of importance for state formation, or the lack of it, in the various regions of the world. In what ensues, we single out the most important factors behind effective state formation in Europe and compare them with the completely different situation in Sub-Saharan Africa, the region containing most of the world's fragile states (state formation in South America and most parts of Asia is not covered). The trajectories to fragile statehood are not simply an African phenomenon, however, and hence the three concrete cases that we then discuss include not only the Congo, but also Afghanistan and Haiti.

The Special Pathways to Fragile Statehood

Modern states in Europe eventually became effective and legitimate, contained robust economies and were composed of nations that were a community of citizens as well as a community of sentiment. How could this happen? Charles Tilly has emphasized that state consolidation in Europe took place in a context of fierce competition and violent conflict; it was the 'continuous aggressive competition for trade and territory among changing states of unequal size, which made war a driving force in European history' (Tilly, 1992: 54). In short, in Tilly's famous aphorism, 'War made the state and the state made war' (Tilly, 1975: 42). It must be remembered that state formation in Europe took place against the background of a long period of fragmentation. In the Middle Ages, power was disjointed and personalized without the formal political and administrative organization of the Roman Empire. Public power was privatized and centred on individuals who took control in military, judicial and economic matters. The power of kings increased between the sixteenth and the eighteenth centuries; that process laid the foundation for the modern state.

Kings grew stronger because of changes in military technology and organization; large armies became a necessary basis for power. This required substantial resources, which kings acquired by beginning to tax the estates and the bourgeoisie. Tax collection called for something to be delivered in return; kings and their fledgeling bureaucracies created a monetary and legal order with a reliable system of credit, a guarantee of the value of money and a legal framework for commodity exchange. Capitalist expansion was greatly facilitated and the bourgeoisie came to accept the burdens of taxation.

Emerging European states also helped each other increase their power in relation to all other actors by creating a special international society of states. The year 1648 was a landmark in this respect: with the Peace of Westphalia that ended the Thirty Years' War, states confirmed their independence from religious authorities and their right to sole control of their internal affairs. States, so to speak, sent a message to all possible rival centres of authority and power – religious as well as secular – that they were in charge and they set the rules of the game for everyone else. Domestically, the consolidation of state power involved the submission of rivals. Before the modern state, persons at the bottom of society were subjected to several different authorities: as Christians, they were subjected to priests and bishops; as peasants, they were subjected to various local, regional and national rulers. With the concentration of power and authority at one point – the king and his government – peasants and Christians became the direct subjects of the king. They became 'the people'; domestic law and order erected a barrier separating the population of the sovereign from the outside. A notion of common purpose could now emerge: the good of the state and the good of the people depended on mutual support and shared obligation towards defending and supporting the state. Obligations (taxation, military service) became combined with citizens' rights of protection and (later) political and social rights. Because of the intense competition with other states, such elements as nationalism and chauvinism were also components of the European process of state formation.

The combination of the state's coercive power, in terms of controlling territory and people, with infrastructural power, in terms of being considered lawful, just and legitimate by the population, is peculiar to Europe. An effective state was created in China much earlier (221 BC) through a long process of intense warfare, but it was based on coercion and not on the rule of law and accountability to citizens. Egypt and Persia are two other examples of very early processes of state making. Two major factors help account for the situation in Europe. On the one hand, the ancient Roman state had a system based on law. Roman law included civil law, regulating exchange and contract relationships between private citizens; public law, defining the rights and duties of citizens towards the state; and criminal law, designed to keep the lower classes under control (Anderson, 1974). On the other hand, the

Catholic Church built on, and further developed, the civil law tradition of Roman law in the attempt to strengthen its position towards secular rulers. The Church did not have armies; it had to appeal to legitimacy and law. But this also provided secular state builders with a model of law and bureaucracy to imitate and extend (Berman, 1993).

Economic development in Europe took place in tandem with the processes of state formation as states created a national space for economic development by removing local barriers to exchange and supporting both industry and infrastructure. At the same time, long-distance trade became increasingly important from the sixteenth century with improvements in shipbuilding and navigation. But states could probably not have created the new capitalist economies on their own. Two other sets of factors were in play: as Marx stressed, the material conditions in Europe facilitated the necessary provision of capital and labour, while, as Weber stressed, ideas played an important motivating role in the form of a Protestant ethic for capitalist expansion.

In Sub-Saharan Africa, the situation was completely different and the processes which characterized the European and Asian societies and states described above did not occur to any major extent. In pre-colonial Africa, there was no competition between rulers for control of territory. The scenario from Europe, of states making war and war making states, did not unfold in Africa because the conditions were not the same. In Europe, a relatively high population density (from the Middle Ages onward) made land scarce and important to control. That, combined with technological change, set European war and state making in motion: rulers were anxious to control a secure area, with such control providing protection from external competitors and a zone for internal consolidation. In Africa, land was abundant and rulers did not compete for control of it. Therefore, basic features related to state making did not emerge: there were no clear boundaries and no well-defined property rights. In the absence of the need to control defined territories, there was no investment in bureaucracies, tax collection and permanent military capabilities (Herbst, 2000). Consequently, while pre-colonial Africa contained a large variety of political systems, most of them were segmented or decentralized with a high degree of diffusion of political power.

Pre-colonial economies were overwhelmingly rural. Because peasants depended primarily on rain-fed agriculture and because they were smallholders, they were only marginally integrated in the formal economy. They were not controlled by the state and state policies were irrelevant to them (Hyden, 1980). Nation-building mechanisms were thus absent. Peasants belonged to their local community and nowhere else. Rather than attempting to establish 'domestic' control of populations, African rulers aimed at external capture of other people. Some societies depended strongly on the slave trade within Africa, as well as beyond, before the advent of colonization: '[T]he point of war was to take women, cattle, and slaves' (Coquery-Vidrovitch, 1976: 105).

The colonial powers took no particular interest in the political and economic development of the areas of which they took possession in Africa. They were more interested in maximizing profits, so their focus was on the extraction and export of natural resources, combined with an effort to curtail their cost of controlling the colonies. According to Robert Jackson and Carl Rosberg, the European layer of domination was 'remarkably thin' (Jackson and Rosberg, 1994: 298) during the colonial period. In some places, colonial rule involved building some infrastructure, together with some political as well as economic institutions. But any such measure remained focused on the cities, not on the countryside. The colonial jurisdictions in Africa were created and later redrawn, trimmed down or enlarged – without any consultation with, or consideration for, the indigenous peoples. To fully appreciate the enormity of the resultant political change, one must consider that the nineteenth-century European 'scramble for Africa' reduced some 10,000 polities to forty European colonies and protectorates (Packenham, 1992).

The Congo makes for an interesting case to illustrate these developments because of the nuances it contains in terms of what the colonizers sought to do. The country emerged from the determination of King Leopold II of Belgium to secure for himself a slice of the 'magnifique gâteau africain'. By 1885, with the help of Sir Henry Morton Stanley, Leopold came to control the Congo Free State, composing an area of nearly one million square miles. Collecting ivory first and wild rubber later, Leopold organized an immensely profitable undertaking. He also created a regime of terror and exploitation which Joseph Conrad called 'the vilest scramble for loot that ever disfigured the history of human conscience' (quoted from Meredith, 2006: 96).

By 1908, the Belgian government took charge, in collaboration with business interests and the Catholic Church. Immense profits kept coming in: by 1959, the Congo produced 10 per cent of the world's copper, 50 per cent of its cobalt and 70 per cent of its industrial diamonds. The operation was able to sustain a Belgian administration of 10,000 in the colony (including military personnel). It was small by European standards but by far the most elaborate colonial government in Africa. The Congolese had no rights or political voice. They could hold lower positions in society and the state apparatus, but the Belgians sought to prevent the emergence of an indigenous elite.

The Congolese were thus completely unprepared for independence in 1960. No one had experience of government or political life. Three Congolese held senior civil service positions. There were thirty university graduates and 136 children had secondary education in a country of twenty million people (Meredith, 2006: 93–115). The Belgians sought to control the transition to independence, hoping to continue business as usual. It ended in complete chaos and anarchy. The fact that the leading political figure, Patrice Lumumba, proved both erratic and irrational in his attempt to control the country was of little help. A prolonged period of turmoil ended with the murder of Lumumba in 1961 and, finally, the takeover by Joseph Mobutu, a senior sergeant from the armed forces, four years later. Mobutu ruled for more than thirty years, with devastating consequences for the country.

The new rulers in Africa were closely connected to their societies via ties of clan, kinship and ethnic affiliation. The clients had great expectations of benefits from relatives or friends in government. This paved the way for clientelism, patronage and nepotism. The Africanization of the state took place in a context of political cultures whose members conceived of government offices and resources 'in terms of possession and consumption' (Jackson and Rosberg, 1994: 302). In desperately poor countries, political power was the major source of status and wealth. The new state elites aspired to entertain Western standards of living, irrespective of the actual poverty of the country. African officials insisted on the same level of salaries and perks that had been given to their European predecessors. Pressure from below for access to state spoils produced an enormous expansion of the state administrations in the newly independent countries (Jackson and Rosberg, 1994: 301).

The legal norms and regulations stipulating appropriate behaviour of state officials controlling public resources were residuals of the colonial administrations. They were frequently looked upon with suspicion from the beginning and were, with some exceptions, never taken seriously. Furthermore, no sense of citizenship or expectations of public accountability existed to back them up. Leaders and clients focused on the here and now: the concrete gains from access to scarce public resources. Leaders would particularly take interest in the control of raw materials for export, in revenues from the taxation of exports and imports and in incoming foreign aid. Entrenched leaders became phenomenally successful in this regard. In the Congo – later Zaïre and today the Democratic Republic of the Congo – President Mobutu was reported to have accumulated personal wealth of \$5 billion by 1984, much of it deposited in Western banks or invested outside the country (Young and Turner, 1985: 440).

Even if most of the contemporary fragile states are in Sub-Saharan Africa, they can be found elsewhere as well. Haiti is a case in point in the Americas and it illustrates that there are different pathways to fragile statehood, some of them radically different from the African experience. After a century of French control, rebel slaves fought against French, British and Spanish troops over several years to finally gain victory and declare independence by 1804. A crippling embargo by the three great powers demolished the export economy; when French recognition came in 1825 it was in exchange for an indemnity of 150 million gold francs that saddled Haiti with a heavy burden of foreign debt. US recognition did not follow until 1862 because the Southern slave states were against it.

The leaders behind Haiti's independence quickly embarked on their own violent struggle for power. Political rule was in the hands of a series of dictators, many of whom were killed or forced into exile. The elite remained settled in a fragile situation between, on the one hand, a large population of illiterate and increasingly poor farmers and smallholders whom they attempted to squeeze through indirect taxation of imports and exports and, on the other hand, foreign merchants, bankers and political elites from whom they strived to secure the best possible deals for themselves. The Duvaliers, father and son, Papa Doc and Baby Doc, ruled for an agonizing three decades, from 1957 to 1986. The United States did suspend aid in 1961, but resumed it when Baby Doc took over at his father's death in 1971. Slightly less blatantly oppressive than his father, he nevertheless continued to amass public funds for private consumption.

A new period of provisional military rule finally gave way to the presidency of Jean-Bertrand Aristide, a Roman Catholic priest, elected with a solid majority in 1990. On the one hand, Aristide pursued populist policies of land reform, labour rights and increased taxes on the wealthy, and these policies antagonized domestic elites and worried international supporters as well (Shah, 2009). On the other hand, his followers also used violence against opponents. After a decade of outside intervention in attempts to restore order and civilian rule, Aristide won election again in 2000, but the opposition refused to accept the result. Aristide employed police and paramilitaries against the opposition. He became increasingly concerned with self-enrichment and had close connections to the narcotics industry. Aristide left the country in 2004 (to return in 2011) and Haiti moved to a new period of violent tensions and political unrest.

On the other side of the globe, Afghanistan offers another case of fragile statehood. The area known as Afghanistan today was conquered by the Persian Empires, by Alexander the Great, the Indo-Greeks, the Indians, Turks and Mongols. Afghanistan's multifaceted history is reflected in the heterogeneity of the population, while the division between different groups is accentuated by geography: the Hindu Kush, a 500-mile mountain range between north-western Pakistan and eastern Afghanistan, separates north and south. The largest group, some 40 per cent of the population, is the Pashtun, south and east of the Hindu Kush; to the north, the Persian and Turkish ethnic groups dominate (the Tajik, Hazara and Uzbek).

On the inside, these groups fought among themselves for control. On the outside, Afghanistan had to deal with two rising and competing empires: Russia to the North and Britain (British India) to the East. Britain began an attempt to control the country, which led to three Anglo-Afghan wars between 1839 and 1919. Eventually, the British settled for less than colonization; they succeeded in making Afghanistan a client state through economic and political manipulation. The country became a buffer zone in the 'Great Game' between Russia and Britain. Afghanistan's independence was recognized by Britain only after the third war between the parties, in August 1919.

For a decade, between 1919 and 1929, a modernizing regime under King Amanullah sought to implement 'Atatürk reforms' in Afghanistan, including abolition of the veil for women, education for all and separation of state and religion. He was met by fierce resistance from tribal and religious leaders and was forced to abdicate. By 1973, 40 per cent of the government's income was made up of external aid (Rashid, 2001: 39). Radical elements of the army were behind a new round of reforms in the 1970s. But the militant government was split in contending factions while the religiously conservative countryside rose against it. The Soviet Union invaded Afghanistan with a large force of more than 100,000 in 1979. By 1989, when the Soviet troops finally withdrew, a new generation of fighters, calling themselves Taliban (those who study Islam), had emerged.

What followed, however, was not peace, but another twenty years of war that devastated the country, killed countless people and made refugees out of an even larger number – over five million had already fled during the Soviet occupation. The victorious Mujahideen descended into a state of warlordism which completely split the country into competing fiefdoms where warlords constantly fought each other in a pattern of changing alliances. In October 2001, the United States launched Operation Enduring Freedom, the aim of which was to destroy Al-Qaeda training camps inside Afghanistan. It succeeded in the sense that there are fewer than one hundred Al-Qaeda left in the country (Partlow, 2009) and the Taliban government was replaced. But the Taliban was not fully defeated and has been able to continue to fight against the new Afghan government based in Kabul and the Mujahideen warlord clans have not united behind the US-supported Afghan President, Hamid Karzai. Fighting continues in a country now utterly ruined in economic terms, and deeply dependent on foreign assistance.

Sovereignty and the Ambiguous Role of Outsiders

Fragile states are politically, economically and socially weak entities. In many cases they are ex-colonies settled within the borders established by the colonial powers. The newly independent states in Sub-Saharan Africa rarely exercised effective control over their territories. The populations were divided along ethnic, linguistic, religious and other lines. There was no developed national economy and many people existed outside the formal economy, living in local subsistence economies. Governments presided over weak and ineffective institutions and they were most often in the hands of small elites seeking to exploit their positions to their own advantage.

Under the classical conditions of state making in Europe, briefly summarized above, such weak entities would not have survived. They would have been swallowed by stronger competitors; that process of 'survival of the fittest' was the typical pattern in Europe. But the situation after the Second World

War was completely different: the new superpowers, the United States and the Soviet Union, supported decolonization and the new states' right to sovereignty. Colonialism came to be considered fundamentally wrong, even 'a crime', according to a UN General Assembly resolution in 1960. In short, the new fragile states were supported by a new set of norms (i.e. colonies have a right of independence and sovereignty) backed by the leading powers in the system. As players in the international system, these fragile states were created from the outside, not from the inside. They were created without any consideration of their substance or capacity as states and were thus the result of the 'survival of the unfittest'.

For these reasons, it is of supreme importance for fragile states to have sovereignty: that is, to have received recognition of their territory and government from international society. Weak regimes and self-seeking rulers with little legitimacy facing divided populations, a lack of functioning institutions and frail economies need all the support they can get. Sovereignty offers access to international institutions, including the UN system; it also offers access to economic, military and other forms of aid. Furthermore, sovereignty provides a formal right of control of territory, government and citizens that is a valuable bargaining resource in relation to both insiders and outsiders (Englebert, 2009). Sovereignty means that strong states cannot merely do what they want in the weak, least developed states. Interventions in other sovereign states cannot be conducted in complete ignorance of the rules of international society; such acts of intervention have to be justified. At the same time, domestic rulers are empowered by sovereignty because outsiders are compelled to bargain with them. Mobutu of Zaïre, for example, cooperated with the CIA (Central Intelligence Agency), but he was not merely the agency's puppet. Because of his formal control of Zaïre, his possession of sovereignty, the CIA had to bargain with him over access to territory and so on. Fragile state or not, sovereignty provided Mobutu with bargaining autonomy in his dealings with other countries.

So international society, led by the UN, and backed by the United States and the Soviet Union, in effect issued a life insurance policy to fragile states: no matter how weak you are, no matter how comprehensively unable you may be to create order, security, welfare and freedom, we confirm your right to independence within existing colonial borders. Without this life insurance, the political map of Africa would surely have looked different today. Robert Jackson makes the point: 'Some central governments would have gained territory at the expense of others, some secessionists would have secured recognition and some new or substantially different countries would have emerged. More powerful states would have expanded at the expense of weaker neighbours' (Jackson, 1992: 10).

The peculiar circumstances characterizing the position of fragile states in the international system underline the ambiguous role of outsiders. On the one hand, outsiders have dominated fragile states to their peril: they came as colonizers, interested in surplus, subordination and control. During the Cold War, much intervention in fragile states was not guided by larger concerns of development and democracy. The United States simply supported anti-Communist rulers, including Mobutu, and the Soviet Union (and Cuba) supported 'progressive' forces in Angola, Afghanistan and elsewhere. On the other hand, the international community has been a major supporter of fragile states: it helped pave the way for independence; it has sponsored aid organizations and relief agencies; and it has conducted humanitarian interventions in order to re-establish order and security.

Following September 11, 2001, the change in US foreign policy, supported by a 'coalition of the willing', has had consequences for fragile states. The new priorities concern the threat from terrorism and 'rogue states' with weapons of mass destruction. The United States declared a readiness to make such countries targets of American force. The claim is that the USA has authority, on a global basis, to conduct preventative intervention against states that harbour perceived threats from terrorism and weapons of mass destruction. It is not entirely clear how and to what extent such policies will change under President Obama. The missions undertaken so far, primarily in Iraq and Afghanistan, claim a mixed record at best when it comes to addressing the fundamental problems of fragile statehood.

So there is both a 'Dr Jekyll' and a 'Mr Hyde' role as concerns the record of outsiders' activities in relation to fragile states. The common feature of these two aspects is, of course, that outsiders have dominated and defined the rules of the game when it comes to fragile states. This is a core difference compared with the dominant role of insiders in the classical process of state making in Europe, and in North America and Japan as well. For fragile states, sovereignty is a basic protection against the termination of states and it imparts substantial bargaining power in the hands of state elites. Nonetheless, it does not eliminate the influence of strong outsiders.

Common Characteristics of Fragile State Formation

It is easy to see that the trajectories of Haiti and Afghanistan are, in separate ways, different from what happened in the Congo and the rest of Sub-Saharan Africa. Still, the two countries share core characteristics with fragile states in other places, Africa included. These core characteristics set fragile states apart from the development experience of effective states in Europe and elsewhere. By pointing them out, we can identify the major factors connected to the emergence of weak statehood.

First of all, fragile states possess formal *sovereignty*: that is, they are recognized as formally independent. We have already touched upon this above, but the point bears repeating: fragile states persist because international society wants it that way, in the sense that they have chosen to keep them from being swallowed up by other states in the international struggle for power. In the absence of formal sovereignty, these utterly fragile states could not have survived, not in Africa, not in the Caribbean, not in Central Asia. They would have been carved up and taken over by stronger outsiders. In other words, fragile states owe their continued existence to the 'world culture' of the sovereign nation-state which emerged with decolonization and triumphed with the break-up of the 'Socialist World System' (Meyer et al., 1997). This situation works for strong interests on both sides of the fence: local elites are empowered by having formal sovereignty; outsiders know there is a severe problem, but it is at least 'fenced in' behind a sovereign border and kept from becoming an object of territorial conquest by power contenders.

The second core element tied to fragile states is that these states are *dominated by self-seeking elites* who are not particularly interested in providing security, order, welfare and freedom for 'their' people. They are indeed very much interested in controlling the state as a source of revenue, but they are not concerned with state building as such. They are frequently guided by their own short-term interests in maximizing power and profit, and because of the peculiar domestic and international circumstances that have prevailed since the mid twentieth century, they are able to take advantage of the situation. On the one hand, leaders do not face a nation, a united group of people; they face a strongly segmented population, split along ethnic, tribal and religious lines. Their nearest supporters look for immediate payoffs. The state apparatus over which they preside is rarely able to exercise effective control in the country. But this is not seen as a detriment to the extent that it provides opportunities for striking deals with power contenders to the advantage of both sides. On the other hand, state elites face strong external groups whose demands may have little to do with effective state making and who, to the contrary, may exploit the situation to their own advantage.

This brings us to the third core element: *external domination*. Direct colonial rule came late to Africa; it was moderated by the Berlin Conference in 1884–5, during which seven European powers agreed among themselves on their division of the continent. But there can be no doubt that the colonial period of less than one hundred years profoundly influenced every aspect of African politics and society. The colonial administrators became the ultimate source of power; local leaders had to obey, and had to do so also when their own people objected. At independence, an authoritarian and patriarchal form of governance was bequeathed to the Africans, within territories demarcated by outsiders with no regard for people on the ground. The export-dependent mono-crop economies continued to be deeply reliant on the world market and aid quickly became a primary source of income.

In Haiti, external domination came earlier. The native population was eliminated and replaced by imported slaves and a French-mulatto elite. Formal independence also came early, but the great-power embargo in the wake of the war of independence brought the country to its knees and underlined its continued weakness in relation to outsiders. For the past century, Haiti has been within the sphere of US influence and deeply dependent on US policy and assistance as well as potential intervention.

Afghanistan was always a gateway between civilizations and in that context it has been controlled (or at least occupied) by a large number of different empires. In the nineteenth and twentieth centuries, it was a hostage in the competition between Britain and Russia; then it was caught up in Cold War tensions; and today, it is an element in the Western struggle against international terrorism. None of this has led to much lasting development or to better conditions for the Afghan people.

The situation of fragile states is counter-intuitive to European conceptions of state formation. Recall the classical contribution by Thomas Hobbes in the seventeenth century: in the absence of a state, people will live in the state of nature where anarchy will reign and life will be 'solitary, poor, nasty, brutish, and short' (Hobbes, 1960: 82). With the state (the Leviathan), claimed Hobbes, there will be security and order. Given the experience of fragile states, it is reasonable to inquire as to how Hobbes can claim that the Leviathan will always deliver in terms of effective statehood. Unfortunately, Hobbes assumes away the problem through a strict specification of the demands on the sovereign for protection of people and property. Given the egoistic nature of humans, why would the sovereign meet these demands? Why would the state elite not be as self-interested and power loving as anyone else?

This can be called Hobbes's dilemma (Keohane, 1995). In the analysis of the history of European state formation, two solutions are offered for the task of coping with this dilemma, one realist and one liberal. The realist solution focuses on external threat. The anarchic international system is a self-help system. State elites are compelled to provide for domestic order because, without it, the state will be disabled and powerless when it comes to facing external enemies. This was a crucial factor in European state formation: elites sought to create such domestic order and civility that the state – and thus the regime – would be able to face external threat. It was a core element in North American, Japanese and Chinese state formation as well (Sørensen, 1996). But the mechanism does not work in the context of fragile state formation, and we have seen why: the external threat of extermination of the state is absent. There is a new norm of the right to survival of even the weakest entities.

The liberal response to Hobbes's dilemma focuses on constitutional government: that is, democratic institutions which provide checks on the power of rulers. Ideally, democracy assures that state elites who become predatory will not remain in power and it assures that elites in power are subjected to the rule of law. But democracy does not necessarily provide a quick fix; in a number of cases it took several hundred years to establish the consolidated democracies which today comprise the OECD world. It is extremely difficult to graft democracy onto fragile states lacking the proper institutions and a level of trust and mutual acceptance among contending groups of the elite as well as of the general population. There have been elections and other democratic elements in the fragile states reviewed above, but these states remain quite distant from successful democratic consolidation. At the same time, early processes of democratization mean better possibilities for formulating demands and getting conflicts out in the open; this can easily lead to sharper confrontations and conflicts that can threaten to undermine frail democratic openings. We shall have more to say about this in chapter 4. But for now we can conclude that Hobbes based his analysis on the European experience and that history does not provide a good guide to state formation in fragile states. Fragile states are characterized by peculiar trajectories, different from the European success stories.

Blocked Development and the Persistence of Fragile States

The formal recognition of fragile states implies that there will be no solution to fragile statehood through recolonization. Beyond this basic fact, what is in store for fragile states? Can we expect fragile states to develop politically, economically and otherwise, following in the footsteps of the now developed countries? That is the optimistic liberal modernization view as we explained in chapter 1. We rejected that view, for obvious reasons: liberal optimism is not based on analysis; rather it is an idealist hope for the future. But the future is open-ended, not pre-programmed for travel along a universal path to modernity.

Where does that leave the fragile states? Since the future is open-ended, they are not all doomed, of course. Some of them might succeed in accord with liberal optimism. In chapter 5, we focus on a few countries that, on first glance, 'ought' to be fragile, but have actually succeeded in creating a solid measure of political and economic development. We identify the major reasons for their success.

At the same time, the few successes are exceptions rather than the rule. The vast majority of fragile states are cases of what may be called 'blocked development'. 'Blocked development' is not a situation of complete stagnation or standstill; it doesn't mean that nothing ever happens. What it does mean is that attempts at political, economic and social development are liable to remain erratic: 'one step forward, two steps back', or, in the happier cases, 'two steps forward one step back'.

Take political development. There were democratic openings in many fragile states after the end of the Cold War. They have been replaced by 'standstill', a situation where countries have acquired some components of a democratic system and have even held decent elections, but they have little political participation beyond elections. Elites remain corrupt and self-interested, there is no rule of law and no free press, and effective institutions, too, are lacking. Because the conditions for further democratic advancement are so poor, the fragile states are likely to remain in a gray area between semi-democracy and outright authoritarianism. According to Thomas Carothers, this gray area is 'not an exceptional category to be defined only in terms of its not being one thing or the other; it is a state of normality for many societies, for better or for worse' (Carothers, 2002: 18).

Or take economic development. As exporters of natural resources, fragile states may profit from rising prices on the world market. But these prices are extremely volatile, with serious repercussions for countries which depend very much on export revenues. Absent the ability to counteract world market developments, every improvement of the situation may be followed by a slump, which is indeed the common experience. Also, successes in fostering local production may be corroded by cheap products which are being dumped upon the local markets by the old and the new industrialized countries. Fragile states have little leverage to deal with this situation. As a result, Africa even witnessed a downturn of its GNP in the late 1970s and in the 1980s. In other words, there was a process of negative growth over almost two decades. During that same period, external aid was donated to these states at extraordinarily high levels. By 2003, the average African country, excluding South Africa and Nigeria, received a staggering 18.6 per cent of GDP in development aid (UNDP, 2005). By comparison, the Marshall Plan aid at its peak amounted to 2.5 per cent of the GDP of countries such as France and Germany. In other words, there has been no lack of external economic aid from which the fragile states of Africa could have benefited. But the result so far is barely visible, if visible at all. Kate Jenkins and William Plowden argue that the most fragile states 'are not by any standards suitable candidates for external help, and donor resources would inevitably be wasted' (Jenkins and Plowden, 2006: 155). This is to say that the neediest are those countries which have the least capacity to absorb development assistance. This conclusion is well known within the development community. But no breakthrough for the better is in sight, despite serious efforts to learn from past experience.

Therefore, the fragile states will be present for some considerable time into the future. We need to understand why they generate so much conflict, and what, if anything, outsiders can do about it. It is these issues which we investigate in detail in the chapters that follow.

CHAPTER THREE

Fragile Statehood and Violent Conflict

This chapter explores the linkages between fragile statehood and violent conflict. We situate our contribution within the large debate about the subject. A first set of analyses on the linkages has focused on issues related to identity (i.e. ethnic cleavages, religion, language, culture) as the central causes of violent conflict (Brown, 1997; Kaldor, 1999). Cleavages related to identity can aggravate conflict between different groups, but that need not always be the case. We argue that ethnic and other socio-cultural divisions become important in generating violence in conflict; it is when political leaders successfully politicize them and rally people around them that they induce people to become violent.

Struggles over economic resources have been a second focus concerning the cause of violent conflict. In fragile states, most people are poor. When poverty leads to crisis because of increasing scarcity of resources, fragile statehood may be accompanied by violent struggles over economic resources. At the same time, countries with abundant resources may experience more instability and violent conflict because struggles over the control of these resources intensify (Berdal and Malone, 2000). Struggles over scarce or abundant resources often aggravate conflict. But again, we argue that the resource issue is an enabling factor rather than a basic cause. It is when resources become elements in a political struggle that they can fuel violent conflict.

Our focus, then, is on the relationship between structure

and process. To paraphrase Charles Tilly's (1975) well-known formulation with respect to European state making introduced earlier: fragile states make violence and violence makes fragile states. State fragility in this regard is both a cause and a consequence of violence. The inability of fragile states to maintain a Weberian monopoly of violence is crucial. The monopoly is continually pursued and challenged. In challenging and defending the monopoly, violent means are used. This violent self-help continually undermines the legitimacy of the state. Contending actors in fragile states tend to set in motion self-perpetuating processes of 'violence breeds violence'. Outsiders have frequently contributed to this interaction of state fragility and violence, through colonialism, their direct interventions since independence and as a consequence of uneven globalization.

Our case studies are the Democratic Republic of the Congo (DRC), Afghanistan and Haiti. While all three are fragile states, the countries represent different varieties of the interplay between fragile statehood and violent conflict. The DRC exemplifies conflict in a large fragile state richly endowed with natural resources which have been the object of foreign interests since the beginning of colonization. Afghanistan epitomizes conflict in a middle-sized fragile state with a decentralized system of governance which for centuries has functioned as a transit area in which cultures have intersected and external interests clashed, not over economic interests, but over the country's strategic importance for the entire region. Haiti presents a case of conflict in a small fragile state in which politics continues to oscillate between the poles of emancipation and outright banditry, on the one hand, and external exploitation of the situation and serious attempts to help the country out of its predicament, on the other.

The three countries all fall within the group of the top twenty fragile states presented in chapter 1. In all three, state fragility is accompanied by protracted violence. All three of them tell a story of bad governance by self-seeking elites interacting with local tensions and clientelist patterns of politics. This set-up provides a zero-sum frame of political conflict that leads to a spiral of social disintegration and civil strife. In all the cases, the state has become a source of insecurity rather than the source of security.

The likelihood of violence does appear to be higher in fragile states than in more stable ones. More than two-thirds of the most fragile states (see Table 1.3 in chapter 1) have, since the end of the Cold War, been afflicted by communal strife, rebel raids (sometimes based in other countries), coups, violent uprisings and other forms of violent conflict, but there are a few exceptions (e.g. Cameroon, Malawi, Burkina Faso and Tajikistan). We do not argue that there is a deterministic, law-like relationship between state fragility and violence. Nevertheless, the abundance of violent conflict in many fragile states calls for analysis. In what follows, we further comment on the debate about this relationship; we then turn to the three case studies.

The Debate about State Fragility and Violent Conflict

Many observers have claimed that the violence characterizing the 'new wars' in fragile states derives from the politics of identity (for an overview, see Kaldor, 1999). References to cultural identities are based on common ancestry, a common history, a shared culture, attachment to a specific territory and self-awareness of forming a group (Brown, 1997). This has a mobilizing effect, both directly and indirectly. It is this attachment which may turn identity into an element in political struggles. But it happens only when political entrepreneurs employ cultural identities to sort out friend and foe, and mobilize groups into turning against one another in a process of escalating conflict (Fearon and Laitin, 2000).

This is what happened in the Balkan wars of the 1990s, especially in multicultural Bosnia. Partly as a result of being mobilized to brute terror against other ethnic groups, people strongly identified themselves along ethnic lines and took sides in the ongoing struggle. As this struggle became more and more violent, identification with one's own group was both a matter of survival and a basis for revenge. It was not group affiliation as such that led to violence, but this affiliation was politicized and became an important amplifier of violence. In short, ethnic dividing lines were used in the pursuit of clashing attempts to access power and in turn became the defining factor in identifying friend and foe.

How is it possible to manipulate or seduce people to violent hostility towards groups that used to be peaceful neighbours? Three elements appear to be in play (Thorstensen, 2007). First, there is a nexus of material interests and identity in the context of insecurity. In fragile states, there is an absence of responsive and effective state institutions. Individuals are thus compelled to turn to ethnic, tribal or similar communities for meeting their basic needs. When the ethnic group comes to be considered 'the only possible "safe haven"' because 'people are left with no protection but the solidarity of their kinsmen' (Braathen et al., 2000: 18), identity and material interest combine to become a powerful source of mobilization.

Second, political or cultural leaders may manipulate historical and cultural symbols in combination with the use of brute force, as happened in the Balkan wars. Leaders succeeded in manufacturing a discourse which strongly rallied people around their particular group identity in distinct contrast to other groups. If people were not willing to follow the newly established pattern, they were then forced to take sides, either by exposing them to direct violence or by frightening them through terror. Finally, grievances (perceived injustice, frustration, loss) can drive violent ethnic conflict when they are framed as discrimination against some groups to the benefit of other groups. As we discussed in chapter 2, lack of social integration and political cohesion is a characteristic of state fragility.

In fragile states, clientelist or patronage networks maintain patterns of inclusion and exclusion and control the distribution of valued goods (power, recognition, wealth). Serious efforts to overcome these deficiencies through nation building frequently lead to new violence by those who believe that their identities and the privileges tied to them are threatened. As a consequence, enduring violence and demands for shared power or autonomy by minority groups go hand in hand in fragile states.

We turn next to the role of economic resources in violent conflict. Ironically, as noted, both resource scarcity and resource abundance may lead to conflict. In the latter case, Paul Collier and Anke Hoeffler (2001) have suggested the existence of a 'resource curse': a condition in which countries with abundant resources may very well experience more internal instability and violent conflict than countries with fewer resources (cf. Berdal and Malone, 2000). Three causal mechanisms are at work. First, those who are excluded from the ability to exploit the nation's resources (but who suffer from the ecological consequences) may be tempted to assert themselves by force. Second, violence may result from the greed of certain groups who want to misappropriate the resources of a country for their own material benefit. Third, the availability of resources may be used by rebellious groups (as by governments) to finance and sustain a violent struggle over political power. In other words, state fragility may be regarded as offering special causes of, and opportunities for, the violent appropriation of natural resources. At the same time, the availability of natural resources may enhance state fragility by weakening state institutions because (ironically) elites may believe there is no need to build up an effective tax system in order to attain the necessary revenue. It may also undermine attempts to diversify the economy (Fearon and Laitin, 2003: 81).

Mary Kaldor (1999) has argued that underlying this set of relationships is an *economization* along with a *privatization* of war. *Economization* connotes that economic considerations (calculations of possible gains and risks) have gained in importance as discrete motives for the use of force, while *privatization* refers to the increasing importance of non-state actors in wars (Keen, 2000). Both are linked to state fragility. However, these economic factors do not replace or dominate the political contestation. It is true that in protracted conflicts economic interests may acquire a life of their own, which may make it even more difficult to end violence, but they have not replaced the political processes at the core of the conflict. Given that fighting over resources always involves the issue of distribution and justice, 'resource wars' are highly political and cut deeply into the very fabric of state–society relations (Jung, 2003). We argue that in fragile states, economic interests are more likely to prolong a war than to cause it. Large-scale protracted violence is more likely to come about when fragile statehood is accompanied by the availability of resources, the control of which helps to finance the violence. However, even in conditions of resource scarcity, parties to conflict have found other means by which to overcome their limited military resources. One particularly appalling choice has been the wide-spread recruiting of children in ongoing wars in fragile states as a means of securing the supply of soldiers and of economizing the war effort. Child soldiers are far less expensive than adult recruits and help to fight wars even in conditions of resource scarcity.

The 'privatization of wars' means the 'outsourcing' of military functions and violence by state authorities through the hiring of security firms and mercenaries (Wulf, 2005: 36). The symbolic presence of these forces undermines the state by demonstrating its lack of a monopoly of violence even as these private forces 'support' the state. In addition to outsourcing, there are a considerable number of non-state actors involved. But the state is always involved in one way or the other, even in seemingly autonomous forms of traditional conflict resolution (Hagmann, 2007).

In sum, identity issues and struggle for economic resources are important elements for understanding violent conflict in fragile states, but they are enabling factors rather than primary causes. We want to focus on the political processes that generate and perpetuate violent conflict in relation to the structure of fragile states. It is to this structure/process perspective that we now turn.

A Structure/Process Perspective

The provision of security, which includes the prevention of violence in social struggles, can be regarded as one of the central purposes of statehood. As we have argued above, in fragile states, the degree to which incumbent administrations exercise a legitimate (generally accepted) monopoly of violence is limited. Because there is no assumption that the state will act as a neutral conflict manager, individuals, groups or associations in conflict assert the right to self-help. This is to say, they themselves decide on the means with which they pursue their aims and that the use of physical force is one of those means (Kalyvas, 2006; Trotha, 1997).

Similar to the manner in which self-help works at the international level, self-help at the state level – especially in the form of warlordism – may provide advantages to specific actors in the short term, but tends to perpetuate overall insecurity in the long term. This is so because self-help is accompanied by a general expectation of violence which then functions as an incentive to both strengthen one's own capacity for violence and/or to ally oneself to those who can increase one's capacity. These actions are reciprocated and the cycle is self-reinforcing and self-perpetuating. We may speak of an insecurity dilemma characterizing fragile states (Migdal, 1988; Schlichte, 2008) which parallels John Herz's (1950) classic security dilemma in the international system. An early analysis of the insecurity dilemma in weak states was provided in a series of essays edited by Brian Job (1992); the concept itself was suggested in that volume.

The insecurity dilemma emerges from the paradoxical situation that, on the one hand, fragile states are relatively free from external threat; their continued existence is guaranteed by international society. On the other hand, the fragile state itself poses a serious security threat to major parts of its own population. In a basic sense, anarchy is domesticized: there is an international system of relative order with fairly secure protection of the borders and territories of fragile states, and there is a domestic realm with a high degree of insecurity and conflict. As seen from the perspective of the populations of fragile states, this is an insecurity dilemma because they cannot know what to expect from the state. So they turn to self-help, which, again, reproduces the insecurity to which it responds. At the same time, strategies of outright resistance to, or support of, clientele networks may be counterproductive in terms of achieving security, too.

Ideally, the government's primary task should be to provide security for its population, but instead in the fragile state the government often is the greatest potential threat to people within its boundaries. For this reason, groups may fear that others control the government and may use its resources (the army, the secret police, the courts, economic influence) against them. The result is that the search for security motivates groups in divided societies to seek to control the state or secede if the state's neutrality cannot be assured. Obviously, these efforts exacerbate the situation, because one group's attempts to control the state will reinforce the fears of others, so they respond by competing to influence and even control the government (Saideman et al., 2002: 106–7).

In this context, state–society and intra-societal relations become shaped by the search for power and security by political and social actors. To the degree that rulers are fearful of strong opponents capable of challenging their claim to authority, they may believe it is in their own interest to actively prevent, or passively abstain from, the build-up of a strong security sector. In this sense, the insecurity dilemma may result in a further 'security paradox' (Howe, 2001): weak security forces may be regarded, at least by some incumbent governments, as causing less insecurity than strong ones.

Likewise, citizens might fear systematic suppression from a strong police/security force more than they might fear the insecurity resulting from a weak force. Further, strong political and social actors may believe that this general insecurity gives them a degree of freedom of action which they would not enjoy under the conditions of the functioning monopoly of violence and a corresponding system of accountability and control characteristic of the ideal Weberian state. Therefore, they, too, in this sense may prefer insecurity to security. Similarly, warlords who prosper under state fragility may have a considerable incentive to prevent a strong security force.

Finally, states and sub- or non-state entities (such as communal administrations and social associations) compete for control over their respective constituencies (Migdal, 1988, 1994, 2001). This competition may take the form of shifting coalitions among elite groups based within state institutions and societal associations at the national, regional or local levels. Under these circumstances, self-help may be regarded not simply as anarchy but as the basis for a particular kind of social order (Clapham, 1993; Hagmann and Péclard, 2010).

For example, in the Philippines, the national constitution calls for the dismantling of all paramilitary groups outside the national army. In spite of this provision, there are more than 130 private armies or private armed groups. They are run by a plethora of actors, such as drug lords, smuggling lords, gambling lords and business lords. Their strength derives not only from the barrel of the gun, but also from how they interact with the political structure of the Philippines. The strongmen control the local security situation. But many of them are also tied to the regional and national elites.

The strength of the local strongmen is heavily dependent upon their connection to the national elite. The national elite channel money to the local strongmen as a reward for certain 'services' provided: for instance, by fighting rebel groups. This money can then be used by the local strongmen to strengthen their capacities at both the local and national level. In this way, a network of mutual protection and support emerges and a combination of force and funds produces a specific form of governance. Consequently, the warlords and their armies may become a part of the political system which constitutes and supports the state (Kreuzer, 2009). At the same time, the situation is a highly unstable one which may result in an escalating process where violence breeds violence.

Outsiders play an ambiguous role in this context. In colonial times, the self-conception of European colonialism as a 'civilizing mission' implied that the colonial powers saw themselves as dealing with uncivilized people(s). This helped to legitimate the use of force. European colonialism was rife with violence. Colonial interests were rigorously pursued, sometimes through deepening, and at others through inventing, ethnic cleavages in the service of indirect rule. The resulting patterns of social control constituted a heavy legacy for the post-colonial states. Some of the linkages between fragile statehood and violence outlined above reflect this colonial heritage. In addition, violence was often the result of retaining colonial borders which did not reflect pre-colonial social relations or identity groups.

In general, political independence was not the outcome of long-term changes in the form of state and nation building within the colonies. Independence rather was often the starting point for such efforts. Given the combined pressures of limited time, of cultural cleavages deriving from colonial politics and boundaries and of a shortage of human capital, this was an extremely difficult task. This contributed to the build-up of political and social tensions within the post-colonial states, and these tensions were rife for escalation into open violence. The tasks of state and nation building and the maintenance of security were as often supported by outside interference and outright intervention as they were complicated by it. During the Cold War, external engagement projected East–West competition onto the Third World. This had multiple and often conflicting effects. On the one hand, it curtailed self-determination. On the other, it offered the national elites a chance to attain financial resources and weapons as payment for supporting one side or the other. The extension of the Cold War, at least indirectly, by providing resources in the form of funds and material, supported the emergence of violent forms of self-help and social control within the fragile states. In addition, as we discussed in chapter 2, interstate politics provided a normative frame for upholding claims to sovereignty even where states lacked the substance of statehood.

Instead of working to mitigate violent conflict, East and West frequently used it for their respective purposes. For example, in the 1970s, in most South American countries, social unrest was attributed to the activities of 'international communism'. This served as a pretext for state rulers to justify the repression of social struggles through military rule. The response to unrest was accepted and tacitly supported by the governments of the West because it supported their aims in the larger East–West struggle.

Since the end of the Cold War, there has been increasing competition both among and between the old industrialized countries and the big emerging countries of the South for global resources and markets. These geo-strategic interests may once again trump the international community's interests in advancing democracy and good governance. The same logic may be seen in regard to combating terrorism. The interest in strengthening fragile states may be superseded by the interest of securing the cooperation of any government pledging assistance in fighting 'global terrorism' within its borders. External actors may thereby continue to reinforce patterns of fragile state repression and violence by supporting the current status quo because fragile state leaders link internal threats to their rule to the 'war on terror' (Duffield, 2001; Stohl and Stohl, 2007).

The neoliberal politics which has driven globalization since the early 1980s has also been, at least in part, responsible for the increasing virulence of state fragility as observed since the early 1990s. As Christopher Clapham argues, '[T]he dynamics of the global system itself have undermined the mechanism . . . through which states have to be maintained' (Clapham, 2003: 44). As a result, the post-colonial state is suspended in an ever tighter web of international norms and guidelines which do more to undermine the authority of the existing political order than to provide the foundations for more effective statehood (Schlichte, 2008: 369).

In sum, while the occurrence of large-scale protracted

violence does not define fragile statehood, it is clear that violence is likely to occur and persist in fragile states. The nature of the political system, the access to resources, the social cleavages and the international environment form the crucial structural basis for the enduring processes of 'violence breeds violence' in fragile states (Brown, 1997).

Linkages between Fragile Statehood and Violence: A Summary

Our reasoning can be summarized as shown in Figure 3.1.

Fragile statehood is widely associated with violence. As a matter of fact, domestic violence tends to be understood as the main characteristic of state fragility. However, the relationship between fragile statehood and violent conflict is not that simple. State fragility seems to function as an opportunity structure for violence. And violence tends to perpetuate state fragility. But the relationship between violence and state fra-

Figure 3.1 Fragile states and violent conflict

gility is not of a deterministic nature in the sense that fragility inevitably leads to violence and vice versa.

With regard to violence, the consequences of state fragility are widely varying. This holds true even for neighbouring countries. In Central America, Guatemala, El Salvador and Honduras have high levels of domestic violence merging politics and crime, while in Nicaragua the level of domestic violence is comparatively low (Zinecker, 2009). And even within fragile states the situation can be quite heterogeneous. For instance, in Somalia, parts of the country (Somaliland and Puntland) have managed to remain relatively peaceful and even to develop an autochthonous governance capacity while the rest of the country is torn by violence (Dijkzeul, 2008: 5). Obviously, then, not all state fragility ends up in violence and not all violence reinforces fragility. That is why we have to look into the specific historical trajectories of the interplay between violence and state fragility in order to understand the nature of the linkage.

To examine these linkages between fragility and violence in greater depth, we now turn to the cases of the Democratic Republic of the Congo, Afghanistan and Haiti.

The Democratic Republic of the Congo

The linkage between state fragility and violence is deeply rooted in the colonial history of what is the DRC today. As we saw in chapter 2, this history begins with the explorations of Sir Henry Morton Stanley on behalf of Belgian King Leopold. Leopold claimed the Congo as his own territory. He was formally granted title by the Berlin Conference of 1884–5 and ruled it as his private holding rather than as a colony of Belgium, naming it the Congo Free State. The colonization of the vast territory was financed both through loans granted by the Belgian Parliament and through the sale of concessions to foreign economic entrepreneurs. This led to a pattern of decentralized exploitation of the local population. It disrupted traditional forms of communal life by subjecting the people to brutal, violent and coerced subjugation (including forced labour under slave-like working conditions) and by fostering migration. The initial decades of colonial rule were so abhorrent that European protests pushed the Belgian Parliament into appropriating the Free State from Leopold, declaring it a possession of the Belgian state and renaming it the Belgian Congo in 1908.

The Colonial Legacy
The Belgians controlled and governed the vast territory with the help of an expatriate colonial administration. While some of the most brutal of the practices were reduced, in their almost sixty years of control the Belgian colonial administration evidenced almost no interest in the development of sustainable governing structures. The Congolese were excluded from the administration in order to prevent the formation of an indigenous political elite (Haskin, 2005: 11; Reno, 2006: 46).

As in many other territories with a rich endowment of natural resources, the overall economy of the Belgian colony profited from the rising demand for strategically important raw materials during the First and Second World Wars. On the eve of independence, 'apart from South Africa, the Belgian Congo was the most industrialized and "developed" territory on the continent' (Prunier, 2009: 76). However, following a pattern familiar elsewhere, the benefits of the industry and the extraction of resources were mainly confined to strictly controlled pockets of wealth (large plantations and mines) and flowed to the colonial masters. Further, because of the uneven geographical distribution of the resources, the economic boom led to large-scale labour migration, including migration from Rwanda (which at that time was considered as part of the

Congo Basin) into the north-eastern provinces of the present DRC. After independence, most of these migrants remained in the Congo.

In sum, then, during the colonial period, life in the area of the present DRC was shaped by external forces: that is, the Belgian state and the companies which it invited into the Congo. Both had little or no interest in sharing the management of public affairs with the locals. Instead the locals were made mere objects of external interests and endeavours. The foreign economic agendas resulted in uneven development, which, in turn, enhanced inter-regional economic and social heterogeneity, but also intra-regional social cleavages, especially in the north-east (owing to the migration from the Great Lakes region). In this setting, top-down violence (on the part of the colonial power and the companies) was routinely applied as a practice of social control, which, however, did not provide protection from local violence.

As in many other colonies, a movement for independence gained momentum in the 1950s owing to the disruptions caused by the Second World War, which, in turn, enhanced the emergence of a new critical debate on colonialism in the 'mother countries' and the colonies. The Belgians tried to forestall independence by announcing reforms which allowed for a modicum of political participation by granting permission for the formation of political parties and elections at the communal level in 1957. At the same time, they also tried to quell resistance through force. Both reform and repression served to enhance the drive for independence. Independence was finally granted in 1960. However, as indicated in chapter 2, the Belgian policy of direct rule which had prevented the emergence of trained Congolese administrators resulted in a dramatic lack of personnel available to transform the colonial administration into the political infrastructure of a new state. In addition, because independence came so precipitously, there was no agreement among the various Congolese groups on the main features of the independent state. This led almost immediately to violent struggles over who would control the state.

Independence was preceded by a national election in which more than two dozen parties took part. The leaders of the two most powerful groups, Patrice Lumumba and Joseph Kasavubu, represented two competing concepts for the future of the new state. Lumumba envisaged a strong central state together with a leftist political programme, while Kasavubu proposed a decentralized model with a stronger political role for the local tribes. There was hope that the electoral outcome would lead to indirect power sharing as Lumumba and Kasavubu became Prime Minister and President, respectively. Their attempts to find a workable agreement for the future of the state were complicated by the fact that the Belgian withdrawal showed no concern for the need for an orderly transition. The resulting chaos was exacerbated by the quarrels among the various political factions. In this context, the south-eastern resource-rich province of Katanga, whose resources had been exploited by the mostly Belgian and British-owned Union Minière du Haute Katanga, declared its independence. This action was soon followed by secessionists in Kasai, another resource-rich province in the south-east. The secessionist movements threatened to strip the newly founded state of its most important resource base.

The quarrels between the two factions, the attempts at secession and the behaviour of outsiders ended up in a civil war in which centralists, federalists and separatists fought each other with considerable foreign meddling. This intervention constituted one of the most infamous episodes of post-colonial politics. Lumumba was brutally murdered in January 1961, apparently with the help of foreign secret services. The Secretary General of the UN, Dag Hammarskjöld, who risked much in trying to turn the country away from war, was killed in a plane crash in September the same year under circumstances unsolved still today. The war finally was brought to a close in 1964. However, the underlying conflict over the structure of the new state and the political representation of the various factions remained unresolved.

The Institutionalization of Violence
In 1965, General Mobutu came to power through a coup with the support of the CIA. He attempted to give his personal rule an air of authenticity and a mythic past by renaming the country Zaïre. He introduced a new currency, the zaïre, and ordered government officials to wear non-Western attire he invented for this purpose. The traumatic experience of the preceding war, the suppression of open rebellion and the modicum of public order achieved under his reign earned Mobuto the initial support of significant parts of the population. However, this did not lead to an end to the internal security dilemma outlined in the first part of this chapter. Before long the people began to suffer from the dictatorship's erratic repression and maladministration more than they profited from the limited public security that was provided. While those who managed to obtain and maintain a government position had the chance to benefit from the continued exploitation of the country's immense natural riches, the majority of the Congo's population did not. As in the colonial period, the benefits of this exploitation continued to flow to the international companies, and now they also benefited Mobutu and his clientele. Reminiscent of Belgian King Leopold in the nineteenth century, Mobutu increasingly regarded the national economy as his private property and amassed a huge fortune.

The authoritarian road to development which was touted by the Asian countries (Taiwan, South Korea, Singapore) and which some Western observers found promising for Mobuto's

Congo, too (Reno, 2006: 45), in fact quickly turned into a simple system of predatory self-help in the Congo. The ensuing patronage enabled Mobuto to maintain his grip on power, but did not result in national economic development. During the Cold War, the West acquiesced to corruption, the lack of accountability, clientelist politics and bad governance. This helped to obstruct the political and economic development of the country. Though Mobutu was not particularly popular in the West, he still was supported as a bulwark against Soviet attempts to gain influence in the country. The Congo, in turn, served the West as a rich source of strategically important natural resources such as uranium and copper.

Mobuto's rule in the Congo epitomized the model of the neo-patrimonial state based on a combination of personal rule and a state apparatus geared towards upholding and expanding untrammelled enrichment on the part of the President and his clientele. The Congo returned to King Leopold's idea of a private state and it exhibited the same features: extreme exploitation of the people; fear and mistrust and attempts at self-help on the part of those who wanted more than they already had and on the part of those who felt left out or who were left to their own devices in local conflicts. With the state not playing the role of neutral conflict manager but rather an agent of Mobutu and his clientele, violence played an important role in regulating public affairs. During the Cold War, all this was closely interwoven with Western interests in staying in the country and keeping the Soviets out.

While Mobutu's personal rule had a limited territorial reach, he managed to rule the country through the 1980s without major outbreaks of internal violence. But because of the limited territorial reach of Mobuto's power, he increasingly depended on the assistance of his Western allies, particularly the United States. This was also due to the fact that conflicts in neighbouring countries regularly spilled over into the

Congo from all sides. In the south, the US-supported National Union for Total Independence of Angola (UNITA) used the Congo freely as a rear base and transit area. Similar intrusions occurred on the north-eastern and northern frontier with regard to conflicts in the Great Lakes region (Uganda, Rwanda and Burundi) and Sudan.

Contexts of Violence: Cracks in the System or a System of Cracks?
After the Cold War, when there was no longer a Soviet threat, the United States and the West withdrew their support in line with the new emphasis on good governance, a liberal market economy and democracy promotion as integral parts of Western development cooperation. At the same time, conflict in the adjoining countries escalated and the cracks in Mobuto's system of rule widened. The economy went into a downward spin and seriously undermined the continuation of clientelism. In 1993, the army, now being paid with almost worthless money, turned to robbery and pillage. When the army raided the capital, the entire country was brought to the brink of anarchy. Finally, in 1994, the spillover from the genocide in Rwanda dealt the Mobuto regime its death blow. Hutus fled in great numbers to the Kivu provinces in the north-east of the Congo adjacent to Rwanda, where former Hutu migrants from Rwanda were still living. The huge refugee camps served as a basis for Hutu militias attacking Rwanda and its new Tutsi government under the leadership of Paul Kagame. Mobuto backed the Hutu militias. This provoked an invasion by the Rwandan Patriotic Front (RPF) aimed at dissolving the refugee camps, crushing the militias and capturing those Hutus whom they considered responsible for the genocide. The ensuing armed hostilities constituted the so-called first Congolese War (1996–7), in which Uganda also was involved because it hoped to confront the Lord's Resistance Army

(LRA) operating in the north of Uganda and taking advantage of safe havens across the borders in Sudan and the adjacent Congolese north-east.

The war toppled Mobuto and led to the reinvention of Zaïre as the Democratic Republic of the Congo (DRC). The decisive factor was the presence of Rwanda's RPF in the north-eastern provinces, which strengthened the domestic opposition in the Congo under the leadership of Laurent-Désiré Kabila, who then toppled Mobuto. However, soon after Kabila had replaced Mobuto, he turned to the same predatory behaviour, violence and clientelism that his predecessor had employed. As a result, numerous new conflicts broke out which were fuelled by changes in the political constellation of the northeast. In 1998, the Tutsi-Banjamulenge, the former alliance partners of Kabila in the fight against Mobuto, concluded that they were not adequately represented in the new political administration or in the army and rebelled against Kabila. This 'Second Congolese War', in which millions of people directly and indirectly lost their lives and even more lost their homes and possessions, resulted in Kabila himself being toppled and replaced by his son Joseph Kabila. Thus, intra-Congolese power struggles intersecting with foreign interests (both regional and global) gained a new momentum. Though many of the actors involved were 'non-state' or 'private' political entrepreneurs, it would be premature to see this struggle as a prime example for the 'privatization' and 'economization' of war in the context of state fragility. As a UN Report on the illegal exploitation of natural resources of the Democratic Republic of the Congo (2002) clearly showed, state and non-state actors as well as political and economic issues tend to be inextricably linked. The exploitation required large-scale planning and organization. It was driven through the cooperation between top army commanders and businessmen making use of pre-existing government structures. The consequences were: 'a) a massive availability of financial resources for the Rwandan Patriotic Army, and the individual enrichment of top Rwandan military commanders and civilians; and b) the emergence of illegal networks headed either by top military commanders or businessmen. These two elements form the basis of the link between the exploitation of natural resources and the continuation of the conflict' (UN, 2002).

The study identified the various links between members of governments and the military, on the one hand, and the special firms and smuggling networks controlled by them, on the other, and named more than 150 firms, organizations and individuals involved in the economic exploitation of the conflict. Yet, greed came to bear only in the wake of political agendas. All the foreign participating parties had their own agendas on what to do with internal conflict and political legitimacy. Rwanda was trying to cope with the aftermath of the genocide. Uganda hoped to be able to end the civil war in its own northern territory by fighting the LRA in the Congo. Zimbabwe's Mugabe sided with Kabila Sr in order to win external support for his increasingly shaky government. The political regimes in Angola and Namibia, too, hoped to improve their domestic standing by cooperating with Kabila. Under this perspective, the economic interests fuelling the war were taking advantage of an essentially political contest. This illustrates the argument made in the first part of the chapter about the primacy of the political in violent conflicts. While economic interests certainly contributed to the escalation of conflict and the continuation of violence, the internal political causes of the conflict, including the lack of power sharing at the national level and the inadequate representation of military coalition partners, were paramount. As the war dragged on, economic interests in continuing the violence increased, but the key to the war's continuation in the north-eastern region of the DRC was that the fighting was the means by which to exert

political power and affirm the claim to representation of
Kabila Sr's coalition partners in the political system of the
DRC.

Similarly, social cleavages in the form of ethnic differences served primarily as instruments of political struggle
rather than being the causes of such struggles. It was not the
ethnic difference as such but the politicization of ethnicity
which contributed to the violence. In the 'First' and 'Second
Congolese Wars', the politicization of ethnicity came to bear
heavily in the escalation of conflict into large-scale protracted
violence. The legacy of the early migration from Rwanda into
the Congo Basin in colonial times enhanced the projection of
the conflict behind the genocide in Rwanda onto Congolese
territory. In addition, local resentment between those who
consider themselves as the original population and the
migrants from Rwanda as well as that between pastoralists
(Hema) and farmers (Lendu) was mobilized for conflicting
political agendas. The escalation of these conflicts was driven
by the merger of local issues with the larger political struggle.
Séverine Autesserre even argues that, 'from 1999 onwards,
most violence took place behind the official frontlines' around
'local agendas' (Autesserre, 2009: 257). Thus local agendas
nevertheless are tied to regional and national agendas.

The case of the Congo illustrates a seeming paradox. The
more fragile a state is, the higher are the stakes for the competitors for power in controlling it. Under Mobuto, belonging to
his clientele was the only way of providing for one's own physical and material security, though there always remained the
threat of falling from Mobuto's favour and of even being killed
if that happened. This precarious situation also functioned as
an incentive for enrichment in the post-Mobuto years. The
excluded had 'the choice' to try to duck where they found cover,
to be victimized or to join a militia and be included in the spoils
by participating in exerting violence rather than simply suffer-

ing from it. Violence was internalized as something that did not only happen, but also was made to happen routinely as a means of regulating social relations. However, insecurity bred further insecurity and pulled social and political actors in the Congo away from what should have been their common interest in creating a security-producing state.

Mobuto's attempt to invent a nation (Zaïre) by linking the present to an invented imaginary past was easily recognized by the population merely as a device to claim legitimacy for his rule. Laurent-Désiré Kabila, in turn, employed the rhetoric of 'national liberation' to mobilize a Lumumbist mystique in support of his claim to authority but also failed to provide a basis for national legitimacy that was convincing to the population. Currently, the formal stated commitment to democracy by Joseph Kabila is thus far largely simply a paper promise. If anything, it helps keep the clientelist system functioning. To paraphrase Gérard Prunier's (2009: 360) reading of the Congolese predicament, loyalties do not go to the state as such but have remained divided among a myriad of identities. Citizenship in the formal sense is only one of these. The state lacks both legitimacy and money. Legitimacy remains the larger problem because even when the Congo has generated income from its vast natural resources, the state has remained weak. Yet, in spite of the lack of political and social integration, there seems to be a strong sentiment in favour of keeping the country united. Fear of the dismemberment of the DRC even appears to exceed concerns about security. Pierre Englebert offers this explanation of the puzzle about how the converging interests of the various factions and competing interests within the population function to keep the Congolese state intact:

> For Congolese elites, state sovereignty is a paramount force, which allows for the transformation of the weak state into an economic resource and dwarfs the potential returns of

alternative agendas of self-determination. ... As a result, violent rebellions revolve around the terms of the rebels' integration in the state rather than over the nature of the state itself. Populations at large, on the other hand, value the continued existence of the state despite its abuses, because it offers a structure of predictability that is not associated with guerrillas, warlords or secessionist movements. (Englebert, 2003: 6 and 9)

Consequently, despite the continued violence and the thus far unending wars on its periphery, there are strong internal and external preferences for maintaining the Congolese state. It continues to function as a source of income for the internal elites irrespective of the capacity of the state institutions to perform the public function assigned to them. And it remains the source of legitimacy for multinational corporations and other states that require contractual arrangements to maintain their business and political agreements. The Congo, then, is the story of a state that was born with a legacy of misrule and the self-seeking behaviour of the elites. Its enormous resources were plundered in colonial times and provided a reservoir for continual plunder by new self-seeking elites which emerged victorious after the respective civil wars. These elites in turn used ethnic divisions to fuel domestic violence in lieu of any strong foundation of legitimacy. The outsiders have fuelled this violent cocktail through economic and military support and arms as well as incursions on the external borders of the country.

Afghanistan

The Historical Emergence of Afghanistan as a Fragile State
Afghanistan is the prototype of a fragile state, having never been a fully formed national polity. It has also never been fully under the control of any other state. The country (or rather the

geographical space in which Afghanistan is situated) always has been a place which people from the outside found worth fighting over precisely because nobody seemed to fully control the territory. This is not to say that statehood never has been an important issue in Afghanistan. On the contrary, one may interpret the history of the country as a constant struggle over statehood between those who have attempted to create a central state and those who have resisted any such attempt. Tragically, until today, this struggle has been accompanied by a considerable amount of violence. In this sense, Afghanistan tells the same story as the Congo but in a different way. Here security has been associated rarely with a central government, but rather most often with local subgroups.

Each effort to form a central state in Afghanistan's history has been met with violent resistance. A myriad of sub-state groups have attempted to retain their independence by working against centralization, and by attempting to gain control of the centre as a means to strengthen their own position in the overall political system. In other words, paradoxically, the fighting over the control of the centre was driven by the desire to retain a decentralized structure. This decentralized structure both strengthens and is reinforced by the local identities of the population. Thomas Barfield (2010) argues that it is one's *qawm*, or local population and ethnic group, which dominates daily life in Afghanistan.

As discussed in chapter 2, state formation in Afghanistan may be traced to the invention of a kingdom in the area of today's Afghanistan in the mid-eighteenth century. Until then the area was formally a province under Persian rule. In 1747 when the Persian ruler was assassinated, Achmad Khān Abdālī, a commander in the Persian army who later renamed himself Achmad Shah Durrani, seized the opportunity and opted for independence of the region from which he came. The dynasty which he founded lasted until 1973. Although

Durrani's empire was not called Afghanistan and its boundaries were not identical to the present country, in retrospect we can see that it functioned as a focus for the emergence of Afghanistan in its present shape and that it established the pattern of its history. The new leader immediately led his forces to conquer areas of what is now Eastern Afghanistan, including the Kabul area.

The Durrani Empire was a loose federation of tribes and principalities which did not care to become subjects of central control. The tribes and principalities insisted on their independence and were prepared to fight to maintain it. In addition, tribal coalitions competed with the Durrani for power. After the death of Achmad Shah, various Durrani clans fought among themselves over the persistently contested issue of succession. As a result, the Durrani Empire decomposed into various regional centres of power, turning Kabul, the 'capital' of the Durrani Empire, into but one of the regional power centres, even as it continued to claim a special status as the centre of the kingdom.

State building in the modern sense of the word was initiated by King Abdur Rachman in the late nineteenth century. Abdur Rachman introduced a nation-wide tax and formed a standing army intended to be loyal to the centre. In this the groundwork for a state was laid. Abdur Rachman's nephew, Amanullah, inspired by Kemal Atatürk in Turkey, attempted completion of this work in the 1920s. He introduced schooling, gender equality and equal rights irrespective of religious or tribal associations. However, these reforms provoked violent resistance within the provinces. Pashtun tribes and Tajik militias played a crucial role in the ensuing uprising. Nadir Khan quelled the uprising in 1930 and placed himself on the throne as Amanullah had left the country during the unrest. Nadir Khan abrogated most reforms, though he retained schooling for boys (from which the

Pashtun were exempted) and equality before the religious law.

Nadir Khan also provided an incipient national physical infrastructure, including school buildings and cross-country roads, but no additional major reforms were attempted. Nonetheless, the state remained the focus for the ambitions of many political actors in the country. A new wave of innovations was attempted under the favourable external conditions of the 1950s and 1960s when the political leadership in Kabul cleverly instrumentalized the Cold War to attain support from both sides for their projects. Schooling was expanded, roads were built, factories were created and the army was modernized. In addition, a fairly liberal constitution was adopted under the new King, Sahir Shah.

But what was on paper was one thing, how things were being done quite another. The King ruled with the help of favouritism and corruption in Kabul. No political infrastructure was developed for the integration and representation of the various provincial and tribal interests and preferences at the national level. The modernization agenda was left to a very thin political class of Kabul-educated intellectuals. The politically most active among them were the Communists. Their main antagonists were political activists with a Muslim background.

There was little substantive progress and the King's grip on power weakened as the resentment in the country grew against the political ambitions of the centre. In 1973, the King was toppled by Prince Da'ud, who aligned himself with the Communists. The reform programme which emanated from this coalition provoked new violent protest. When Da'ud tried to adjust his course by turning towards the West, he was ousted and killed by his former Communist associates. The ensuing attempt to enact an even harder top-down approach to modernization provoked fierce battles among the

Communists and between the Communists and the Islamist groups. The end result was the intervention by the USSR in 1979, a disastrous war of attrition culminating with the eventual retreat of the Soviets ten years later.

With regard to the factors which we identified in the first part of this chapter as linking state fragility and violence, political struggles over the control of the centre interacting with external influences were decisive in triggering violence. External influence exerted itself in different ways: on the one hand, it interfered directly with the internal power struggles; on the other hand, it provided impulses for modernization and indirectly fed into these struggles by framing the various issues involved. During the time of the Cold War, external influence led to a partial reframing of social cleavages in religious terms (Eastern and Western modernizers versus Muslim opponents). But religious factors and ethnic heterogeneity played only an auxiliary role as the basis for claims to legitimacy in the ongoing political struggles and for the mobilization of support.

From Fragile Statehood to War

The Soviets withdrew having failed to overcome the resistance of the various Afghan militias and warlords supported by Pakistan, Saudi Arabia and the United States. Following their departure, these militias, often rivals during the war with the Soviets, soon began to fight each other over the agenda of post-war state building. This fighting quickly escalated into an outright civil war. The struggle originated in the regional and local rivalries of the various warlords in the north and in the Pashtun region in the south. It soon engaged an ever-increasing number of groups fighting over both their autonomy and, consistent with Afghan history, which group would control the centre. At first, the fighting concentrated on Kabul (which was all but destroyed) and then later extended to large parts of the countryside. In 1996, after four years of war, Kabul was taken by the Taliban, an Islamist group under Mullah Omar. The majority of the original Taliban were Pashtun from Kandahar who had been educated in Islamic colleges (madrassas) in the border region between Pakistan and Afghanistan (partly under the surveillance of the Pakistan secret service, the ISI). Many of the Taliban were refugees from the civil war and veterans of the struggle against the Soviet troops. The Taliban sought the establishment of the unity of Afghanistan under a fundamentalist reading of Islamic law (Sharia). They gained wider public support when they managed to put an end to some of the factional fighting and raiding among the Mujahideen (Schmeidl, 2009: 71). While the Taliban gained control of the capital, however, this never extended to the entire country. At the pinnacle of their power, they ruled over between two-thirds and three-quarters of the territory. The most important remaining opposition was the Northern Alliance, formed as a last-minute attempt to contain the Taliban.

While public security improved in the areas controlled by the Taliban, individual freedom suffered in a way that consciously and openly violated basic human rights, including religious freedom, tolerance and respect for the cultural heritage of humankind (as illustrated by the destruction of the statues of the Buddhas of Bamiyan in 2001). Decentralized violence was thus replaced by centralized violence. For non-Pashtun people, especially in the big cities, the reign of the Taliban resulted in their subjugation under Pashtun standards of public morality (*Pashtunwali*), which the Taliban elevated to the law of the land. Since the centrifugal forces throughout Afghan history have been so strong, the establishment of a central authority depended on a strong ideology provided by the fundamentalist reading of Sharia. This was also to gloss over the ethnic identity of the Taliban, which, in turn, helped them to shield their power.

With the help of the Northern Alliance on the ground, the Taliban were ousted by the United States in response to the terror attacks of September 11, 2001. (The Taliban were targeted for having shielded Al-Qaeda.) However, the quick ejection of the Taliban from Kabul did not end the fighting. Over time, the Taliban regrouped their forces and soon were back confronting not only the Americans, but also NATO, which functioned as the core of the International Security Assistance Force (ISAF) commissioned by the UN.

When the Taliban took over Kabul in 1996, they had managed for a short moment to tip the peculiar balance of strength and weakness in favour of strengthening the central state. However, they did not build a state; they usurped what they found in terms of a state bureaucracy and security sector and used it for their own purposes. There is no consensus on whether the Taliban actually want a stronger central state or rather are interested in keeping up the moving balance of centralized and decentralized violence in order to have maximum political leeway in pursuing their own ends (Rashid, 2001). But even so, their programmatic commitment to establishing an 'Islamic state' and the claim of legitimacy attached to this claim drove them towards a form of centralized control which in turn in the Afghan context was to be expected to provoke renewed resistance.

State Building as War Making

Afghanistan, then, offers a striking example of how state fragility and violence may re-enforce each other. This interaction calls for a closer look at the political struggles which have shaped the history of the country. The persistent inability of one of the contending groups or any coalition to gain the upper hand, to institutionalize its rule and to turn it into a political system capable of claiming legitimacy is at the bottom of the protracted violence. This violence, though used in an instrumental way, functions as a causal mechanism for its own reproduction. Put simply, the political history of Afghanistan demonstrates how violence breeds violence. However, this is only half of the story, as is evidenced in the manner in which warlords and the militias under their command use their power in pursuit of political and economic resources and interests. The warlords are in violent competition of rival groups from other areas of Afghanistan. They act to maintain their grip on power through both the application of force and the creation of some form of public order in the area they control. This evokes some degree of loyalty from the people and the militias and thus reduces the costs of retaining power. However, to the extent that they levy some form of informal tax or extortion, they double the tax burden the population already has to carry. Thus, there is an element of predation attached to warlord polities. Antonio Giustozzi argues that warlords 'may also team up with war profiteers and "rogue capitalists" in order to develop their own shadow logistics and financial services' (Giustozzi, 2009: 19–20). However, such a relationship is diffiault to consolidate and legitimize. It tends to be confined to periods of acute war. 'After that, warlords either turn into "Mafiosi" or are forced gradually to drop their dangerous liaisons and clean up their act if they want to reinvent themselves as politicians or statesmen' (Giustozzi, 2009: 19–20). At times, this may also lead them to attempt to expand their reign beyond the immediate geographical area they control and to gain the upper hand over the central state. Conversely, warlords may fear that the conquest of the state would undermine their claim to legitimacy, which is essential for the perpetuation of their leadership. As a result, they may also prefer to rely on their sub-state basis of power. Under this perspective, the Taliban did the right thing. They combined a comprehensive ideology (their reading of Sharia) meant to support their claim to power at the centre with their ethnic/regional background as a reserve source of strength.

As in the DRC, the warlords in Afghanistan may develop economic interests detached from their self-understanding or from the aims they profess to serve. However, drugs aside, Afghanistan has generally had less to offer to warlords than the DRC with its rich natural resources. The economy has traditionally consisted of subsistence agriculture, with corn, rice, barley, wheat, vegetables, fruit and nut production along with cotton and tobacco as major crops produced in the country. While there are potentially lucrative natural resources, including minerals, precious stone deposits, natural gas and petroleum reserves, they have not as yet been exploited in a systematic way.

A significant issue in Afghanistan is to what extent violence springs from the inability of the state to provide for a functioning national economy. The economic progress during the 1950s and 1960s did not lead to a sustainable economic diversification. Rather, it facilitated rent seeking on the part of those profiting from the rivalling development assistance granted by East and West in the context of the Cold War. Many of the economic projects introduced under the scheme of development assistance did not pay heed to the developmental needs of the country but rather reflected the perceptions and preferences of outside actors. They also heightened external dependency. The two decades of war destroyed the little that had been achieved in terms of economic development at the national level. In sum, the Afghan state never succeeded in providing basic public services to the population, and the attempts to use external aid to help jump-start such a process have not fared well.

Complicating these questions in the current period is the role of opium. In the past three decades, opium has become a crucial part of the economy. Prior to the mid-twentieth century, there was no significant opium production in Afghanistan. However, following the Soviet invasion, the opposing warlords required a cash crop to generate the revenue necessary to purchase weapons, and opium initially filled that need. The warlords and the Mujahideen organized the market for opium production and promoted opium cultivation in the areas under their control. The result was that Afghanistan became the world's largest producer of the drug. While the Taliban sought to reduce opium production, one of the consequences of their ouster in 2001 was that this once again dramatically increased. The Karzai government, requiring the support of the warlords, turned a blind eye to the drug production and trade. The UN Office on Drugs and Crime estimated that in 2007 opium accounted for 35 per cent of Afghanistan's GNP. This has had a pernicious effect on the rule of law as the opium trade supplies significant profits to both the warlords and many in the central government. These profits generate the funds available for weapons and for distribution to supporters. Drug production thus profits the central government (as well as the warlords) but simultaneously corrupts the foundations of the central state. Opium becomes a resource that both the government and the warlords have an active interest in furthering, and this in turn strengthens the criminalization of the political system and further reduces trust in the state.

Of course, in dealing with the frequency of violence in Afghanistan, the socio-cultural traditions of the country are significant. In this respect, the clan-based conception of honour is of special importance as a basis for social rules. Rules describe the duties of an honourable life. These duties include the use of force in the defence of those for whom one carries responsibility. It extends to the defence of the family, the village, the clan and the nation. Acting in the defence of honour is bound to a rigid code of conduct, and taking the law into one's own hands. In Afghan society, the feud is a central component of the system of assuring justice (Kessel, 1968) and is part of a broad consensus on ideals which legitimize the use of force by the parties to a conflict (instead of relegating it to a third party like a court or the police). This socio-cultural norm is reinforced by the continuing weakness of the institutions of the central state. In view of the many conflicts that exist between the sub-state polities, one should expect a continuation of the use of violence in any conflict involving the issue of honour and the accompanying duties. In Afghanistan as in other countries, large-scale violence does not simply *emanate* from the cultural features of social formations. It involves mobilization and organization. The ability to provide for both is part of the *raison d'être* of the warlord polities in Afghanistan. Ethnic differences among the very different groups are used to build legitimacy for local rulers, and violence has been an endemic part of this legitimacy for a long time. A local warlord gains legitimacy and following because he provides some measure of security for members of a certain ethnic group. The result has been a situation where violence towards other groups has become endemic.

From the Outside In: Interference without Transformation
As already pointed out, in Afghanistan, the violent rivalry among sub-state polities must also be understood within the context of external influence and intervention. Though the country never was a colony, contemporary Afghanistan may be considered in part as the product of British colonialism and the British struggle against rivalling interests on the northern flank of British India. It was the resistance against British intrusion which fostered the rudimentary political integration of the area for which the foundation had been laid one hundred years earlier at the creation of the Kabul kingdom. After two disastrous defeats, the British agreed to a semi-

autonomous status of the area. This marked the beginning of the Afghan state of today. The state-building activities of Abdul Rahman were financed by the British, who hoped to oblige the King to keep the Russians out in return. As mentioned, the outburst of economic activities in the 1950s and 1960s grew from the rival activities of the Soviet Union and the West to increase their influence in the country as part of the Cold War. The Soviet intervention provided the next push for closer cooperation among the various factions. Finally, the Taliban could not have organized and been as effective in dealing with the warring Mujahideen without external assistance. Utilizing connections established during the war against the Soviets (Yousaf and Adkin, 1992), the Taliban were trained, advised and actively supported by the Pakistani Secret Service (ISI). One of the driving forces behind Pakistani policy was the rivalry with India over influence in the area (Rashid, 2001). After the initial defeat of the Taliban by the American Operation Enduring Freedom (OEF) in 2001, Pakistan offered itself as a stronghold in the Western 'war on terror', while at least part of the ISI continued clandestinely to support the Taliban.

There is general agreement that the nineteenth-century birth of an Afghan state in its present shape was achieved at the price of a birth-defect which continues to trouble the country today. As part of the deal between Abdul Rahman and the British, the border was drawn between Afghanistan and British India (the Durand Line) so as to deliberately cut through the Pashtun settlement areas in order to weaken them politically and economically. The legacy of this decision is that the contemporary border area between Pakistan and Afghanistan is not only part of the current war zone but also an area in which insurgents in both countries may be granted safe haven.

In sum, we end up with a complex image of the Afghan

legacy of state fragility and violence. The Afghanistan case illustrates how the use of organized violence develops a dynamic of its own. The rivalling attempts by both warlords and the state to provide security have resulted in a society where violence and war has been the norm. In one sense, the sustained use of organized violence always relates to the Afghan state. It is around the ambitions of gaining control of the state and thereby achieving security or preventing the state from threatening your local security that much of Afghan history is shaped. Afghanistan is a weak state whose sources of weakness enabled it to resist all attempts even by world powers to control the political evolution of the country. The great powers managed to interfere but they did not manage to transform. The inability of first Britain, then the USSR and now NATO and the USA to achieve this transformation has been due to the fact that while their internal counterparts either had no real interest in state building or were too weak to achieve it, they were strong enough to spoil external attempts to act as proxies for internal reformers.

So in the case of Afghanistan, the weak state manifests itself in strength: the strength of the numerous Afghan tribes and clans and their militias. This strength results from the determination of the provincial chiefs, warlords and other subjects of collective violence to defend their independence. The military capabilities of these actors are directed against both foreign intruders and intrusions by the central state into what they regard as their 'domestic' sphere. In this sense, one can speak of Afghanistan's 'weak state and strong society' (Saikal, 2005). The strong local society is the source of the weakness of the state and the weakness of the state helps to perpetuate the autonomy claims of the sub-state collective actors. However, fighting for one's own independence has increasingly also involved fighting over the control of the centre. Fighting over the centre, in turn, inadvertently upgrades its political weight and indirectly fosters claims for a stronger state. In this way, defiance of the state and state building continue in violent conjunction. Afghanistan is a prime example of the domestic security dilemma. When a weak central state cannot provide security, local actors step in and thereby further weaken the fragile state. Outside attempts to re-create state strength under those circumstances become difficult, to say the least. We will return to the outsiders in the next chapter.

Haiti

For Sixty-Eight Years, What Have We Done? The Legacy of the Long Post-Colonial Struggle
Haiti was the site of the first European settlement in the 'New World'. It was also the first colony within Latin America and the Caribbean to achieve independence, through a successful revolution in 1804. Independence was accompanied by the abolition of slavery. Nonetheless, in its more than two hundred year history as an independent state, Haiti has remained poor, violent and riddled with catastrophes, including failed revolutions and protracted repression, external meddling and internal strife, hurricanes and earthquakes, famine and floods. Haiti illustrates how violence is institutionalized by elites fighting for control of the state or clinging to power once they have achieved control. It further illustrates how social or ethnic cleavages can be employed to fuel fear and violence.

This history was not predictable or predestined. Until independence, Haiti was the most prosperous of the French colonies, but its prosperity was achieved on the shoulders of slaves. The vast majority were born in Africa and composed about 90 per cent of the population. They were ruthlessly exploited and brutally treated. The French colonialists calculated that it was cheaper to maintain and expand the work-force by importing new slaves than by treating them decently and allowing them to reproduce within the country. The remainder of the population were approximately half-mulatto (*gens de couleur*) and half-whites. While the mulattos had certain rights, including the right to own land and slaves, they were a class subordinate to the white colonists.

In 1791, groups of slaves began to revolt against the French colonial administration. This had happened before, but this time it occurred in the wake of the French Revolution, which sent messages of freedom and emancipation across the Atlantic. Fired by these messages, the revolt turned into a long and bloody struggle for independence, which, after a brief interim period of peace and relative prosperity under the '*homme de couleur*' Toussaint Louverture, was finally achieved in 1804. The struggle in Haiti had repercussions on the Americas and beyond. The newly independent country assisted Simón Bolivar in the initial phase of his fight for Latin American independence. More importantly, the Haitian struggle provided a historic push to the international campaign against slavery. Tragically, however, the emancipatory message of Haitian independence did not carry very far in the country itself. With the declaration of independence, the leaders of the armies that had beaten the French colonial forces proclaimed their Commander-in-Chief, Jean-Jacques Dessalines, Governor-General of Haiti for life and granted him extraordinarily wide powers. This move steered the country down the wrong path in its initial years. In this respect, one can speak of a certain path dependence of politics in Haiti's post-colonial history. As in the DRC more than a century and a half later, there were at the time of independence few people capable of running a state administration. The first post-colonial generation of political leaders only knew how to make war, but not how to make a state. This had serious consequences. Dessalines was a courageous man with remarkable military skills. But he was not an administrator.

'He had no qualifications for civil rule, and his administration degenerated into a tyranny under which he and his officers systematically exploited the people' (Davis, 1928: 98). The consequence was that the victorious military struggle did not produce a viable political system capable of representing and integrating the various social groups in the country. It opened the way for a protracted struggle among those who prospered, those who wanted to get a better deal within the system and those who contested it.

Under Dessalines, the plantations seized from the French were distributed to the military and the favourites of the new ruler. They were now worked by the freed former slaves. The rent paid by them effectively tied them to the estate in an informal serfdom under which the colonial whip was replaced by the *coco macaque*, a heavy cane for the punishment of the recalcitrant. This provoked a post-colonial rebellion in 1806, during which Dessalines, who had proclaimed himself Emperor, was killed. In the struggle over his succession, the small country was split between a despotic north and a liberal south. In a sense, they represented the two sides of the French Revolution: its emancipatory impulse and its dictatorial backlash under Napoleon. The north was run by Henri Christophe, a hard-liner who came to power with the help of the military. He was a Napoleonic modernizer. In contrast, the leader of the south, Pétion, was inspired by the emancipatory ideas of the Enlightenment and the French Revolution. He was elected according to the rules of a democratic constitution he himself had previously crafted. Christophe pursued a path of autocratic development by building schools, erecting impressive buildings, enhancing commerce and inviting foreigners to improve the local conditions. However, the development was accompanied by atrocious brutality undermining the effort. The south followed a more modest line of development based on democratic politics and small landholdings, created by seizing the lands of the rich gentry, enabling a basic but reliable existence. But near the end of his reign, Pétion turned towards self-privilege. Ignoring constitutional restrictions to his rule, he declared himself President for Life in 1816.

These 'models' existed for more than a dozen years side by side. The country was reunited under Jean-Pierre Boyer, who attempted to integrate the two approaches and to reshape state and society. But he, too, failed and the various dividing lines between the minority and the majority, the haves and the have-nots, the mulatto and the black, the urban population and the peasantry deepened. The gap between poverty, on the one side, power and affluence, on the other, became ever more irreconcilable. These gaps have remained a source of serious unrest all through Haiti's history, though the dividing lines themselves were often blurred.

Within its first few decades, Haiti moved from the most prosperous of the French colonies to become the poorhouse of the Western Hemisphere. The mismanagement and growing predatory behaviour of the dominant class was important to this result, but there were also reasons for the economic decline beyond the control of the Haitians. Since much of the revenue of the government depended on taxing imports and exports, the post-colonial country needed foreign recognition to stabilize its economic foundations. But the relevant trading countries were slave states, and they refused recognition. The government desperately tried to correct this situation through trade talks with its former 'mother country', France. But France exacted prohibitively large payment from Haiti: 115 million francs for reparations and another 30 million francs as payment for the colonial fortifications and public buildings that the French had built (a total of almost $20 billion in today's currency). In addition, France demanded trade conditions from Haiti that greatly decreased the revenues of the country. The reparations were reduced by approximately 60 per cent in later negotiations, but these crippling payments seriously curtailed the capacity of the government to fulfil its functions.

The internal and external difficulties of keeping up the old export-led economy of the French colonial period led to a restructuring of the patterns of land use. There remained some bigger export-producing estates, but the dominant form of land use became subsistence farming combined with a small surplus production for local markets. This had profound economic consequences. With more than two-thirds of the landowners possessing one hectare or less, the plots tilled by the peasants were so small that they could barely feed those working on them and Haiti could not achieve self-sufficiency in food production. To the present day, Haiti has depended more and more on the imports of foodstuffs. But even with these imports, the great majority of the people have suffered from constant food insecurity. Over time, conditions have worsened because of soil degradation and deforestation resulting from the prevailing practices of eking out a living under an increasing competition for land. The ensuing scarcities do not necessarily translate into violence, but they contribute to the political climate in which violence has thrived from the nineteenth century to the present day. The grievances of the poor could easily be instrumentalized by those involved in the struggle for political control.

Within a few decades, a pattern of changing constitutions and governments evolved. Looking at the results of the first seven decades of independence, the Port-au-Prince *Gazette du Peuple* on 6 April 1871 stated in desperation:

> For sixty-eight years ... what have we done? Nothing or almost nothing. All our constitutions are defective, all our laws are incomplete, our custom houses are badly administered, our navy is detestable, our finances are rotten to the core; our police is badly organized, our army is in a pitiable

state; the legislative power is not understood and never will
be; the primary elections are neglected and our people feel
not their importance; almost all our public edifices are in
ruins; the public instruction is almost entirely abandoned.
(cited in Davis, 1928: 130)

Occupation, Domination and Revolt
This pattern was temporarily interrupted by the American
occupation of the country, which began in December 1914
and ended in 1934. The occupation followed a familiar pattern
of external meddling with Caribbean affairs. It was prompted
by the threat of intervention by France and Germany to collect
overdue debt payments and the fear of US government that
the Germans were about to strengthen their political influence in the country. In the spirit of the Monroe Doctrine, the
United States, under President Woodrow Wilson, wanted to
pre-empt such an 'extra-Hemispheric' threat to their interests.
They established a financial protectorate over the country (as
Teddy Roosevelt had done earlier in Santo Domingo). When
the Haitian government refused, the United States sent in the
Marines, who confiscated $500,000 worth of gold deposited
in the National Bank as a first step on the way to the complete
control of Haiti's finances. While the US government claimed
that it had no designs on the political and territorial integrity of
the country, it imposed a new constitution that seriously curtailed Haiti's sovereignty (like the Platt Amendment had done
before with regard to the Cuban constitution in 1903). This led
to various revolts, which in turn were suppressed by the US
Marines. The US occupation led to the improvement of the
physical infrastructure of the country, but it contributed little
to overcoming the existing political and economic development blockages. The occupation buttressed the forced labour
practices that had been imposed by the economic elites. The
tough repression exhibited a snobbish, if not racist, attitude

towards the people. The resulting resentment translated into a sense of nationhood on the part of the Haitians, and the occupation at the same time demoralized an already bedevilled people. When the United States finally withdrew in 1934, the old struggles for power and representation continued until, in 1957, 'Papa Doc' Duvalier was named President by the military. He established a rigidly repressive rule, later continued by his son Jean-Claude Duvalier. The Duvaliers claimed to finally end the subjugation of the majority (the blacks) by a small minority (the mulattos). But instead of improving the representation of 'black' interests within the political system, they terrorized the larger part of the population with the help of the Tonton Macoutes, a paramilitary force established by Papa Doc ruthlessly suppressing all opposition, whether black or mulatto.

As in the entire history of the country, self-enrichment and repression by the Duvaliers bred rebellion. It finally led to the downfall of the Duvaliers in 1986. The period following the end of Duvalier rule was characterized by a return to the old pattern of political unrest, coups and counter-coups. Four years later, however, in the context of the 'third wave of democratization' (Huntington, 1992), there emerged a new confidence that the country was about to undergo substantive change. In 1990, Haiti's first free elections of the twentieth century were held and Jean-Bertrand Aristide, a priest who courageously had resisted the Duvaliers, won a resounding victory. He was supported by a social movement (Lavalas) which called for a fundamental renewal of Haitian society and politics based on the beliefs and values of the peasantry. Aristide immediately pushed through substantive reforms, first and foremost in the agricultural sector, which was of the greatest importance for his followers (with 80 per cent of the population depending on smallholder agriculture). This measure cemented the great fear of and opposition to Aristide among the elite. Aristide's political style exacerbated the antagonism of the elite and, what was even worse for Haiti, created antagonism even from his own supporters in parliament. Aristide's attempts to curtail the political power of the military created a backlash within the security forces and increased the unrest within the country. The hope of the majority of the population that the country was moving in the right direction was rather short-lived. After only seven months in office, Aristide was ousted in a bloody *putsch* and replaced by a military junta. This junta soon became notorious for its involvement in drug dealing and smuggling.

Under the auspices of the UN, an international force of some 20,000 troops led by the United States intervened and reinstalled Aristide as President in 1994. This intervention also cleared the way for new elections in 1995. Formally abiding by the 1987 constitution, which ruled out immediate re-election, Aristide abstained from running. However, he arranged for his closest political ally, René Préval, to run instead. Préval won an even higher percentage of the vote than had Aristide in 1990, although there was a very low voter turn-out. In the subsequent elections of 2000, Aristide ran and attained his second victory. However, he quickly encountered even harder resistance from the traditional power-holders than he had experienced during his first term. This took the form of a civil-war-like situation which brought the international community back to Haiti. This time, Latin American countries acting within mandates of the UN and the Organization of American States led the intervention. During the intervention, Aristide left the country; whether he fled the country or was taken out against his will by the United States remains unresolved. In the subsequent elections of 2006, Préval was again elected and continued as President of Haiti through his term's end in 2011. During this period Haiti remained in somewhat the same situation in which it always had been: economically weak, politically fragile and internationally dependent, as well as at the mercy of large-scale 'natural' catastrophes. The disastrous earthquake of 2010, in its unprecedented attendant destruction and loss of life, did not change the basic pattern of living at the brink which has been a characteristic feature of Haiti from its beginning.

The State as Booty
Haiti continues to witness persistent political instability and irregular violence. A key factor is the opportunism of political actors as they relate to each other. Since the fall of the Duvaliers, most of the political forces have been affiliated with three major political blocs: the neo-Duvalierist authoritarian coalition, the neoliberal reformist bloc and the populist Lavalasian sectors. But these groupings are 'not frozen entities; they are internally fragmented, and members of each can move from one to the other. . . . Dramatic about-faces reflecting very sudden changes of allegiance are common among the political elites and class groupings' (Fatton, 2002: 29). The decisive question, then, is what would cause this opportunism. One answer is that the state, weak as it is, still offers an entry point for establishing for oneself a relatively secure perspective of well-being and influence. Therefore, the elites and political actors are careful to stay close to the sources of state power. On the one hand, there is an incentive to join one of the respective coalitions in order to assure one's presence in the sites of state power. On the other hand, flexibility in affiliations has become a key element of elite political culture lest one ends up on the losing side. This rule seems to work all the way down to the lower end of the social hierarchy where most of the violence occurs. Thus, as Robert Fatton states, during Aristide's second term, the offspring of the Duvaliers, the Tonton Macoutes, were to be found not only among the violent thugs of criminal bands (the Zinglendos),

but also in the Chimère, the militant wing 'of an increasingly militarized Lavalas' (Fatton, 2002: 29). The common denominator of these groups is 'mob rule'. From the perspective of the Weberian state, mob rule would be considered simply as a challenge to the state; but here it may also serve as an instrument of those running the state (Schlichte, 2008). One of the many criticisms voiced against Aristide (both inside and outside Haiti) is that he did not distance himself from mob violence committed in his name. The 'mob' was one of his important sources of support and helped to maintain his political power vis-à-vis the elites.

Haitian culture and the structure of Haitian society are relevant for how fragile statehood and violence interact. Fatton argues that Haiti's violence is 'rooted in the predatory interests of the dominant class' (Fatton, 2002: 51). Anthony Maingot defines this dominant class as the 'elites, both civilian and military, the fifteen percent (all urbanites) who live off the government budgets, and the rapacious *chefs de section*' (Maingot, 1996: 206). One may speak of a 'political economy' of conflict enriched with cultural elements.

The state in Haiti is predatory in nature. Compared to Afghanistan and the Congo, in Haiti the state does not cash in on big rents derived from natural resources or opium. Rather, contributing directly to the continued immiseration of the country, the state extracts revenues from the poor through taxes and fees. These revenues are not transformed into public goods but are simply transferred to those who are in control. In this regard, the state acts as a Robin Hood in reverse. Not all violence in Haiti may be related to the question of who gets what, but the violent struggle often does function in this context.

At various times since the fall of the Duvaliers, it appeared that the violence, instead of serving predatory interests, could also create an opportunity for liberalization and democratization. In this context, Fatton (2002: 32) credits the Lavalas, despite their shortcomings, as a driving force towards change. Up to now, however, such observations and the resulting hopes have regularly been overtaken by set-backs. The possibilities of liberalization and democratization offer new sources of violence, particularly during elections as the outcomes determine how state power will be employed and to whose benefit. Haiti's continual political violence may be seen as a repetition of the patterns emerging from the particular situation under which independence was achieved.

Conclusion

In the introductory section of this chapter, we discussed various attempts at explaining the violence in fragile states. We acknowledged the importance of ethnic and other social cleavages and of economic motives for using force. Our main thesis was, however, that political factors are crucial. Attention should be focused on the way in which elite behaviour and structural features of fragile statehood relate to each other. The absence of an effective monopoly of legitimate force allows for self-help as a way of deciding who gets what. Self-help, in turn, abets insecurity, and insecurity abets the drive towards clan politics, clientelism and securing support by mobilizing ethnic or religious identities or by forcing people to take sides, if necessary by brute force. This practice, again, re-enforces the structural features of fragile statehood.

Our reading of the three cases illustrates how politics works in the context of state fragility. In the DRC and Afghanistan, there is a lack of central control over the territory defining the state. Thus, sub-state, trans-national and international actors step in and link local conflicts to a wider context. In Haiti, the main problem is not territorial but social control. In this case, mob violence becomes an important factor shaping public life. In all three countries, the practice of self-help enhances insecurity and in turn enforces the segmentary differentiation of the societies along clan or ethnic lines. The result is a zero-sum framing of political conflict and the dominance of short-term interests over medium- or long-term considerations. Because of its weakness, there is a permanent struggle over the control of the central state by the various contending factions. This seeming paradox can easily be explained. We have seen that the state may be a source of a relatively stable income (DRC, Haiti), it may be an instrument of the privileged for upholding the public order from which they profit (DRC, Haiti) and it may be used against any attempt to undermine one's own power basis by the many sub-state polities affiliated with state fragility in the first place (Afghanistan). Under these conditions, reformist or revolutionary agendas tend to get lost quickly in the established patterns of doing politics (Haiti, Afghanistan).

At first sight, there seems to be a very strong linkage between economic factors and violence in fragile states. The debate on the resource curse suggests that much of the violence in fragile states is caused by predation. But the three cases have very different patterns. In the case of the DRC, the experience in the 'First' and 'Second Congolese Wars' speaks to the importance of the exploitation of natural resources as an object of war. However, the exploitation of the natural resources was not a causal factor for the fighting; at most, it offered an opportunity structure for extended fighting over the political agendas pursued by the warring factions. In the case of Afghanistan, the economic interests of the various domestic actors are clearly not a decisive driving force of violence, even though economic interests have entered the picture with the expansion of opium production. In Haiti, attaining or upholding economic privileges, on the one hand, and the resultant poverty, on the other, are important background variables for explaining violence in the form of repression and rebellion. But again, economic interests and grievances are tied into a political struggle over who controls the state. Under the Duvaliers, mob violence was part of their system of rule. While some of this mob violence has simply turned criminal, other parts of it, during the second term of Aristide, apparently operated in the political context of the Lavalas. So the three cases would confirm that there is no clear-cut tendency towards the 'economization' or 'privatization' of violence in fragile states.

As far as cultural traditions, ethnicity and the resulting politics of identity are concerned, all three cases confirm the importance of these factors. Political entrepreneurs refer to or practise them in order to enhance their claims to legitimacy and to mobilize support. But they are clearly of an instrumental nature. The Duvaliers in Haiti consciously played up ethnic difference (between the blacks and the mulattos), but clearly and exclusively as a means to enhance their power. Mobuto in the Congo invented cultural traditions in order to provide his rule with an aura of legitimacy. Ethnic or cultural factors seem to be more important in Afghanistan. But even here, the historical experience suggests that violence, first and foremost, is about eking out local autonomy (or shielding it against a usurpation by the centre) and that cultural traditions or ethnic factors play an auxiliary role in the pursuit of this agenda.

As we have seen, outside actors have been part and parcel of the game of fragile statehood in the three cases. They were partners of the ruling elites (during most of Mobutu's time in DRC) and adversaries (during most of Afghan history and US occupation of Haiti), but they also have switched roles (in all three countries). In addition to involvement with the political elites in the three countries, outsiders have provided the global opportunity conditions for both modernization and predation. The question today is whether outside forces can adjust their policies vis-à-vis the ruling elites and help reduce state fragility. With this we turn to chapter 4.

CHAPTER FOUR

Coping with State Fragility

In the preceding chapter, we have considered the role of outsiders as a component of the problem of state fragility and violence. In this chapter we will address to what extent outsiders can become part of the solution. We ask whether outside intervention offers a remedy for fragility and for the violence which, as we have shown, quite frequently accompanies it. We will argue that the capacity of outsiders to address the problems of weak states is limited and that both domestic and international conditions make interventions problematic undertakings. We are not arguing that all external interventions are doomed or that external actors can never do any good. There are cases of both pre- and post-conflict fragile states where extensive international involvement clearly had a stabilizing effect (e.g. Namibia, Macedonia and South Africa). In more general terms, analysts have credited international involvement, particularly UN peacekeeping forces, for the decline in intrastate conflicts since the peak years of the early 1990s (see, e.g., Human Security Report, 2005). However, the number of intrastate conflicts since that report was written, while remaining below the peak years, has levelled off at a still comparatively high rate. The most spectacular cases, Somalia, Afghanistan, the DRC, Darfur, Haiti and parts of the Balkans, still remain unresolved. The future of Iraq, too, remains uncertain, while the recent uprisings in the Arab world leave the international community puzzled as to what to do. Not surprisingly, then, the optimism of the 1990s about the possibilities of intervening in violent intrastate conflicts from the outside has suffered serious blows.

The record of outside intervention in fragile states is rather mixed, to say the least (Bercovitch and Jackson, 2009: 101;Weiss, 2007: 81–6). While some argue that for a number of cases it is still too early to judge (e.g. Kosovo or Bosnia), there are quite apparent fundamental problems related to outside intervention in fragile states which need to be addressed. The most important of these problems relates specifically to military intervention. The experience of the past twenty years indicates that it is extremely difficult to try to break the cycle of violence and to provide the necessary space for peace through the imposition of outside force. It is also quite risky, since the use of force may actually prolong or even aggravate violence, as illustrated, for example, by the cases of Somalia, Afghanistan, pre-Dayton Bosnia and possibly the DRC (Bercovitch and Jackson, 2009: 101; Weiss, 2007: 81–6).

The events in Libya in 2011 illustrate how the international push to 'do something' may lead to military intervention even while the limited options for what to do and how to do it should spell caution. However, the conundrum is that it is not an acceptable option for the international community to stand by and do nothing when people are acutely threatened. The core of the problem is that military intervention is intended to be of a limited temporal nature. In this capacity, it affects the dynamic of a conflict. As we argued in chapter 3, the crucial point is how this dynamic interacts with structural features of the conflict. Military intervention, owing to its very nature as a limited undertaking, is not geared to deal with these structural features. Therefore, there is a tendency to extend interventions much beyond their initially anticipated scope. The result is that the initial concerns of external actors about whether 'to get in' are soon matched by concerns about how 'to get out'. The current war in Afghanistan is a prime example of this. Another fundamental problem is that interveners, whose motives for intervention are not only humanitarian but self-interested as well, confront self-seeking elites who are struggling to preserve their own ruling autonomy and power, and to gain resources for their own wealth accumulation. The interaction of these elites, who often have ties to external actors beyond the interveners, creates a context in which it is extremely difficult for the intervention to address the patterns of intersection between structure and process in violent conflict.

In confronting these issues, we focus primarily on military intervention and examine how the international community has intervened and with what effects during the years since the Second World War. Our focus is the utility of military intervention in contributing to the reduction of violence and the improvement of state capacity. As we shall see, the how, when and why of intervention have changed over time. The adverse domestic conditions which prompt intervention also make it difficult and risky. While the main subject of what follows is military intervention, we will also look at development cooperation. This is a kind of intervention because it feeds into conflict and violence both directly (through military aid as a part of development assistance) and indirectly (by unintentionally helping to finance clientelist networks in the recipient countries). Furthermore, the line between military and non-military assistance deliberately has been made more blurry as part of the new global security agenda (Duffield, 2001). To illustrate the complexities of coping with state fragility from the outside and to place practices of intervention in greater context, we will follow our general discussion with an examination of the international community's interventions in our three case studies of the Democratic Republic of the Congo, Afghanistan and Haiti.

From East–West Competition to Humanitarian Intervention

As we discussed above, some fragile states such as the Congo instantly became part of an emerging bipolar competition between the United States and the Soviet Union. Both superpowers had global ambitions and attempted to recruit other countries to their side. The superpowers dominated economic and political developments within their respective blocs, especially during the first decades of the Cold War. For the most part, the two superpowers and their allies formally respected the principle of non-intervention. In practice, however, when they determined that vital security interests were at stake, they tried to get around the norm, often by arguing that they had intervened to ward off the intervention of the other side. These interventions had the primary purpose of serving the security interests of the superpowers and thus they did not contribute much to mitigating fragile statehood.

What emerged from decolonization, then, was a new type of very weak player in the international system and an easy target for external interference in the context of the Cold War. The former colonies were granted juridical sovereignty in spite of the fact that they contained very little in terms of substantial statehood, politically, economically or as regards nationhood: that is, cultural and political community. They were protected by an international norm of non-intervention (expressed in Article 2/7 of the UN Charter) which fostered the claim of sovereignty regardless of the nature of the state. While this norm virtually guaranteed that there would be no old-fashioned, imperialistic take-over of weak states, as we indicated above in chapter 2, it also allowed for the continued existence of many states that in earlier periods of international history would have disappeared as political entities as they would have been swallowed by stronger competitors.

Many of the newly emerging states had difficulty in fulfilling the basic obligations of statehood to their citizens and were continually torn by instability and violence, with literally dozens of coups occurring in the 1960s and 1970s (see McGowan, 2003; Tillema, 1989). Yet, the end of colonialism as such strengthened the norms of self-determination and non-intervention since the right to self-determination was the central argument for independence (Friendly Relations Declaration of the UN of 1970). East and West acknowledged these in the context of their ideological competition in the South. There was a reluctance of the 'non-African powers to intervene in the affairs of African states without having been invited to do so by their governments' (Jackson and Rosberg, 1982: 17). Furthermore, changes of borders and expansion of territorial control were considered unacceptable in order to avoid a prolongation or initiation of wars of liberation. The assumption was that any change of the new state boundaries must involve the acceptance by the sovereign states affected by that change (Jackson, 1995).

Thus, the international community felt no need to respond if the security problems of the state did not 'spill over' to other states and if the security problems did not signify a shift in loyalties to either West or East. There was little international concern if the state was ineffective in providing basic well-being to its people or if its regime was illegitimate or unpopular as long as the results of these failures did not create 'international' security problems.

When the Cold War ended, there was a sense of a new beginning for international society. The Paris Charter of 1990 called for a community of democracies, including both the USA and Russia. Further, there was a hope that humanitarian concerns would no longer 'belong exclusively to the internal affairs of the state concerned' (Baylis, 1999: 17). In the East, states were now reconstituted on a new foundation of democracy and free markets. In the Third World, a second nation-building process was started (Fukuyama, 1992). Leaders of Western countries perceived a unique window of opportunity to reshape the international system on the basis of liberal economic structures and to institute international society on a stronger, more universally based normative foundation. They believed that the rules of coexistence could now be redrafted (Dewitt et al., 1993).

Pundits and scholars considered it a monumental historic moment. John Lewis Gaddis (1999) described it as a giant movement of tectonic plates whereby new fault lines appeared in the international system's basic rules. In particular, the assumptions about the distinction between what is international and what is domestic were challenged and it was believed that the basic rule of non-intervention would make way for a world society based on universal human rights. It was believed possible that the conduct of states towards their own citizens might now become an important concern for all states. International policy makers were well aware of the magnitude of this shift and wrestled with the implications. Both the United States and the newly re-established Russia expressed their support for a more active UN role in preventing state failures and managing the new order. Ambitions for the UN reached their peak with Secretary General Boutros Boutros-Ghali's *Agenda for Peace* in 1992. A Security Council summit-level session was held for the first, and to date the only time, on the basis of a British initiative in January 1992. The meeting produced three proposals: (1) that the concept of security be expanded to include human rights and human security; (2) that Article 43 on a UN standing army be revisited; and (3) that the composition of the Security Council – and, therefore, the UN Charter – be reformed (Knight and Yamashita, 1993: 308). Global governance seemed to be in the making.

Meanwhile, a number of fragile states experienced failure or collapse. These state failures prompted numerous discussions of the need for crisis involvement by international society. Increasingly, the discussion turned to the need to address the international norms underlying sovereignty and non-intervention. For many, fragile and failed states were believed to be the responsibility of the international community. Failed and fragile states were also seen as a challenge to the ambitions of the liberal world order. There was a belief that the end of the Cold War created new possibilities for international action because UN Security Council (UNSC) decisions would no longer be blocked by the East–West confrontation. The context of what was now labelled the post-Cold War 'moment' created a sense that failure could be stopped and more democratic states with greater respect for human rights could now be created. These beliefs and the occurrence of significant humanitarian crises led to a number of humanitarian interventions in the 1990s, the first of which were the UN interventions in post-Gulf War Iraq to protect minorities from retribution by the Saddam Hussein regime in 1991 and in Somalia in 1992.

The Somalia intervention followed more than three years of civil war which had resulted in the overthrow of the dictator Siad Barre in January 1991. Subsequent to attacks on the appointed interim President Ali Mohamed Mahdi's forces by General Mohamed Farah Aidid's Somali National Alliance in November 1991, international involvement began as an effort to deliver humanitarian aid to the people of Somalia. In April 1992, UNSC Resolution 751 authorized a fifty-man mission (United Nations Operations Somalia: UNOSOM) for food distribution. The United States followed suit with Operation Provide Relief on 14 August 1992 and then, only weeks before President George H. W. Bush left office, announced Operation Restore Hope. This was approved by UNSC Resolution 794 on 3 December 1992, as part of UNITAF, the Unified Task Force for Somalia. In total, 38,000 troops from twenty-one nations were involved, with 28,000 coming from the United States. In their initial engagement, these troops were relatively successful, and in addition to providing supplies, they were able to provide the space for a ceasefire between Mahdi's and Aidid's forces in March 1993.

On this basis, a follow-up mission to UNOSOM was created (UNOSOM II) with the task of not only continuing relief efforts but also restoring peace and helping to re-establish Somali governing institutions. In June 1993, in the context of continuing attacks by Somali militias against UNOSOM II personnel, the Security Council authorized the mission to employ all necessary measures against all those responsible for such attacks, including their arrest and detention for prosecution, trial and punishment. This decision to widen the mission in the context of the deteriorating situation was to lead directly to the deaths of eighteen American and twenty-three Pakistani soldiers in Mogadishu. As a result, President Clinton announced the withdrawal of American forces and declared that a political, rather than a military, solution to the humanitarian crisis had to be found. The US role ended in March 1994, followed by the entire UNOSOM intervention a year later. While the intervention provided some short-term relief, it was not able to help construct a political framework for sustaining order. Partly as a consequence of this trail of events, the UN force was no longer a neutral player and it never succeeded in the planned disarmament of the clans. While the UN estimated that 250,000 lives were saved by the intervention (*Somalia-Unosom II*, 1997), the condition of Somalia as a functioning state was not improved by the three years of military intervention.

The experience in Somalia dramatically affected subsequent considerations of intervention. While the international community had begun the decade with much hope about the possibilities of positive international involvement and the role of intervention, the combination of peacekeepers' deaths and lack of success in Somalia inhibited future military engagements. The intervention in Somalia raised questions about whether international involvement could be designed both to help protect people and stabilize the states affected.

As a consequence, international society as a whole, and especially the great-power members of it, was slow to react in the face of the next major disaster, the 1994 genocide in Rwanda. It came against the background of conflicts between the Hutu majority and the Tutsi minority, which predated independence in 1959 (Prunier, 1995). The sequence of events leading up to the genocide began in 1990 when Tutsis in exile commenced a civil war in Rwanda in an attempt to oust the Hutu rulers. The confrontation led to a negotiated settlement in 1993. A multilateral UN force of 2,500 was assigned to supervise the implementation of the agreement. It was clear from early on that the agreement did not satisfy the Hutus (Clapham, 1996b). After a period of mounting tensions, the Hutu President, Juvenal Habyarimana, was killed when his plane was shot down in April 1994. That signalled the beginning of systematic killing of Tutsis by radical Hutus unwilling to give up or share state power as stipulated in the agreement. Between 500,000 and 800,000 people were butchered in less than a hundred days (Prunier, 1995). The UN forces had reported their fears of impending ethnic killing previously in January 1994 and the Security Council was informed when the genocide began but did nothing for two weeks. Inexplicably, the Security Council then decided to *reduce* the UN presence in Rwanda to a token force of 270 troops to act as 'intermediaries'. Four weeks later, it was decided to deploy a force of 5,500, but the great powers continued to be unwilling to commit themselves to the operation. The actual intervention was basically undertaken by French troops. This intervention only came three months later and functioned mainly as a mission to protect the Hutus (in the country and in the adjacent areas of the DRC) from the revenge of the Tutsis (Knudsen, 1999: 266). UN Secretary General Boutros-Ghali summarized the international responsibility for the appalling loss of human life, 'We all must recognize that . . . we have failed in our response to the agony of Rwanda' (UN, 1994: 11).

The events in Somalia and Rwanda dramatically slowed the ambitions of Western governments to intervene in violent domestic conflict for humanitarian reasons. Their policies towards fragile and failing states, in contrast to the intentions of the Agenda for Peace, were now mostly based on *ad hoc* reasoning in the context of an emerging crisis. The inability to secure a positive outcome in Somalia and the lack of response to the devastating numbers of victims in Rwanda cast doubt on the ability of the international community to intervene constructively or with the needed dispatch.

In Europe, the break-up of Yugoslavia and the wars that followed witnessed the EU states changing from one policy principle to the next without finding a common foundation. At the outset, EU policy was to maintain Yugoslavia intact, but German opposition embarked the EU on a policy of recognition of new states (Hodge, 1999: 181). The EU then undertook humanitarian relief operations in these areas, but took exception to the idea of military intervention outside the UN framework. This position became more and more untenable as the conflict dragged on even after the Dayton Peace Agreement of 1995. The participation of most of the EU countries in the Kosovo war in 1999 was the end-point of a long struggle concerning the need to intervene even without UN authorization (Roberts, 2000). The failure of Dutch UN troops to protect the people in the 'safe haven' at Srebrenica in 1995 was a decisive moment in this struggle.

Thousands were killed under the eyes of the UN. On the US side, the Bush (Sr) administration initially maintained a policy of non-intervention in the Yugoslav situation, a stance that the Clinton administration followed only later to change that policy totally, first by taking the lead in the UN mission to Yugoslavia and by bombing the Serbs to the negotiating table (Dayton Agreement) and then by waging the Kosovo war without UN authorization. Thus, the preliminary agreement on new rules of international action in defence of people's security and human rights evaporated. Some feared that, as in the past, each case would be responded to on an *ad hoc* policy basis and that no clear policy guidelines for conducting intervention in conflict would come forth. Others felt that no such guidelines should be developed (Byman and Waxman, 2000). It was this situation that prompted the Canadian government to create the International Commission on Intervention and State Sovereignty (ICISS), which in 2001 produced a report on the 'Responsibility to Protect'.

The report came in the context of increasing concern about 'new wars' (Kaldor, 1999). In these new types of conflict, the boundary lines between state and non-state actions were blurred, making it virtually impossible to distinguish between crime and politics, random killings and systematic repression. The identification of these 'new wars' was closely linked to the emerging debate on state failure. For many, the occurrence of these new conflicts was taken as an indication of state failure. Therefore, the role of intervention, in addition to protecting people in conflict, was to provide the political space for structural change as a means for overcoming state fragility. This implied a major shift in the way the relationship of peace and development was conceived. In the immediate aftermath of independence, common wisdom had it that peace could be attained within the former colonies through development. After the end of the Cold War, development cooperation took a new turn, with much greater concern for institution building and conflict resolution, which were now seen as preconditions for successful development. This amounted to a move of 'bringing the state back in' (Evans et al., 1985) after state intervention in the economy had been cut to the bone as a condition of the structural adjustment policies imposed in the 1980s and 1990s by the IMF and the World Bank. At the same time, 'the state' had to live up to an increasing number of standards like fostering democratization, respecting human rights and, after September 2001, cooperating in the fight against terrorism. Thus, 'bringing the state back in' went along with efforts to redefine sovereignty such that it tied the exercise of sovereignty to the fulfilment of certain duties both vis-à-vis the people and vis-à-vis the international community (Bothe et al., 2004). This not only facilitated the protection of people in conflict but also fomented fear that new pretexts for intervention were being invented (Brock, 2009).

September 11 and After: The Securitization of Fragile Statehood

The past decade's debate on security and intervention was altered dramatically by the events of September 11, 2001. After the terrorist attacks on the United States, the United Nations Security Council called upon every country to cooperate in the fight against terrorism. While the UN Security Council recognized that the United States had suffered an armed attack allowing recourse to the right to self-defence, the 'war on terror' created significant complications with the passage of time. The war in Iraq, initiated by the Bush administration under the guise of eliminating what were in fact nonexistent weapons of mass destruction and justified by claims of Iraq's ties to Al-Qaeda and the 9/11 hijackers, was recast as a war to install democracy and remove the arbitrary power and abuse of Saddam Hussein's regime. Many state leaders and many state populations, including most significantly France, Germany, Russia and China, did not support the war's justification or the war.

The lack of UN and Western agreement on the justification for the war further muddled the argument over the status of the sovereignty norm in the international system. Critics of the war argued that an intervention may only take place if sanctioned by the Security Council as a necessary though not sufficient precondition for collective military action. In contrast, the United States argued that the 'war on terror' created the right to intervene in order to prevent the development of future threats. This Bush Doctrine was spelled out in the US National Security Strategy of 2002. While the argument underlying the Bush Doctrine was not accepted by the leaders of any of the other major powers, with the exception of the United Kingdom's Tony Blair, it clearly shifted the nature of the ensuing international debate. The terror attacks of September 11, 2001 and the subsequent wars thus set a new context for assessing the importance of fragile states, for understanding what was so problematic about them and for devising strategies for coping with them. Prior to 9/11, the problem of fragile states was viewed at best as peripheral by the new Bush administration. In addition, both inside and outside the USA, few had argued that the problem of fragile states was what Ashton Carter and William Perry (1999) had labelled an A-list security problem. Rather, fragile states (then discussed mainly under the label of failed states) were seen by 'security' experts as a humanitarian concern. The 9/11 attacks, however, orchestrated from within Afghanistan, demonstrated to reluctant foreign policy establishments that fragile states provided opportunities for safe haven for terrorists, for establishing training centres and for massing large numbers of operatives. Those who had not been swayed by the 'humanitarian' arguments as to the importance of fragile states were now convinced of their strategic consequence (see, e.g., Record, 2002: 5; Walt, 2002: 62). In this sense, the importance of political and economic fragility as a possible serious security concern vaulted to the top of many foreign policy agendas.

But that did not mean that the foreign policy establishments now saw all fragile states as a problem. Even within the parameters established by the new national security orientation of the Bush administration, the problems of failed and fragile states continued to receive less attention, fewer resources and less strategic consideration than should have been expected. While the global 'war on terror' saw fragile states as a security threat, it did so in terms of the threats to other states and not in terms of building government capacity, improving economies or managing their borders and tracking resource flows (see Rice, 2003). Thus, while vast sums poured into defence budgets for the promulgation of the war in Iraq, appropriations for the build-up of the governmental capacity and economic development of fragile states in general and Iraq as well as Afghanistan in particular were comparatively small. And while democratization emerged as a belated justification of the war in Iraq, the new additional justification by the Bush administration did not assuage the war's critics and/ or most of the other potential great powers, with the exception again of Tony Blair's UK government. This policy evidenced very little concern with the underlying problem of the fragile state.

During this period, 'international society' also facilitated the involvement of other external actors in weak states: all kinds of arms dealers, smugglers and mercenaries exploited the opportunities that the new unfettered global marketplace allowed (Hartung, 2001). This also did not contribute to effective state building. The combination of the marketplace and the general trend towards privatization and outsourcing of government functions around the world (Singer, 2005) has further exacerbated the problem. Within the context of the new global 'war on terror' by the United States, the weapons shipped to non-democratic and often weak governments continued and indeed expanded, particularly in the Middle East and Southwest, South and East Asia.

To this day, the major trade in arms continues to be dominated by the five permanent members of the UN Security Council in addition to the participation of Belgium, Brazil, Bulgaria, Germany, Israel, Italy, South Africa and Sweden (Stohl and Grillot, 2009). The arms trade and the gray market for trading natural resources against weapons have facilitated the emergence of numerous warlords who strive to control territory, plunder resources and wield power by making the local populations an object of their ruthless ambitions. Major arms-producing countries have often turned a blind eye to both the 'end use' and the 'end user' of weapons shipped, and very rarely effectively control the extensive illicit trade in arms. ('End use' refers to the purpose of the weapons and 'end user' refers to the actual defined user of the purchase such as Country A's military or police force.) While the United States and the United Kingdom, for example, both have provisions within their legislated regulatory systems which prohibit the sale of weapons to gross human rights violators or prohibit the sale of weapons the purpose of which would be to repress populations, their promotion of arms sales often overwhelms their interest in enforcing these prohibitions, as the 2011 report of the UK House of Commons committee on arms export controls so aptly described (Norton-Taylor, 2011).

The reluctance of the international community to deal with violent intrastate conflicts in a consistent manner further complicates the problem of fragile statehood. Not only is the international community reluctant to intervene, but it is still unclear as well as contentious, a decade after the release of the Responsibility to Protect report, under what circumstances, under whose authority and for what purposes interventions will occur, be authorized and implemented, and then according to which achieved goals such interventions will conclude. The protracted discussions surrounding intervention in Libya in 2011 well illustrated these tensions. And even after the intervention was authorized by the Security Council, the members disagreed over exactly what they had authorized.

The New Context for Intervention in Weak States: 'The Responsibility to Protect'

While the international community had been inconsistent in how it responded to intervention in the 1990s, the September 11 attacks also had the effect of derailing the developing discussion within the international community with respect to intervention and the rights of sovereignty. The Paris Charter of 1990 was one of the first examples of how a new notion of sovereignty as both a right and a responsibility began to evolve. Collective security, early warning and post-conflict rehabilitation were key concerns. But the Charter also stressed the commitment of all signatories to human rights and democracy. The developing international debate was further advanced by the revisions of the African Charter contained in the Constitutive Act for the African Union (AU) in 2002. These revisions contained language that was completely absent from the charter of its predecessor organization, the OAU (the Organization of African Unity), from 1963.

The respective stipulations of the AU Charter are an especially vivid illustration of a fundamental change in the perception of what sovereignty means to states. African states had been the most resistant to questions of intervention in the sovereign affairs of another state. Thus, for example, when Julius Nyerere of Tanzania was asked about his role in deposing Idi Amin of Uganda in 1980, he argued that he (and Tanzania) only had responded to Uganda's aggression against Tanzania and he refused to assert a Tanzanian right to protect the citizens of Uganda from a murderous dictator. Instead, Nyerere emphasized that the Tanzanian state respected the principle of non-interference and that it remained overriding in importance. Thus he stated, 'I never fought to get rid of a tyrant. I fought an aggressor. I got rid of an enemy' (see Stohl, 1987: 157).

Against this background, it is all the more remarkable that Article 4 of the 2002 Charter of the African Union gives the right to this organization to intervene in a member state pursuant to a decision of the Assembly in respect of grave circumstances, namely war crimes, genocide and crimes against humanity. The Preamble declares that promotion and protection of human and people's rights, the consolidation of democratic institutions, and good governance and the rule of law are part of the objectives of the Union. However, the same Constitutive Act has retained much of the language of the former Charter of the OAU when it comes to the protection of the sovereignty, territorial integrity and independence of its member states. In Article 4, it is also stressed that there is a prohibition on the use of force and of interference by any member state in the internal affairs of another. Thus, the 2002 Constitutive Act for Africa reflects the normative coexistence at the international level of both the norm of the international protection of human rights and the norm of non-intervention. They are, in fact, placed side by side in the act.

Nevertheless, the differences from the 1963 Charter are illustrative of the normative change that has taken place in the past half-century. In the 1963 Charter, there was no right to intervene, but rather an obligation to eradicate all forms of colonialism from Africa. In addition, Article 3 underlined that the member states should show respect for the sovereignty and territorial integrity of each state and for each state's inalienable right to independent existence.

This change in normative thinking (though not yet in actual practice) is confirmed by the 'responsibility to protect' (R2P). This formula in a nutshell represents the argument of the International Commission on Intervention and States Sovereignty (ICISS) discussed earlier. The Commission was set up in the wake of the Kosovo war. In its final report, it attempts to clarify the basic issues underlying the shortcomings of humanitarian intervention. The ICISS argued that the international community had the duty to protect people in conflict from gross violations of human rights. This duty went along with the responsibility to prevent such violence and to rebuild a war-torn country after a ceasefire agreement has been attained. The basic ideas were considered by the High-Level Panel on Threats, Challenges and Change, which UN Secretary General Kofi Annan convened in November 2003 in preparation for a reform of the United Nations. Annan strongly believed that it was important to address the lack of agreement on the proper role for the international community in providing security to people in conflict. And the report of the panel endorsed 'the emerging norm that there is a collective international responsibility to protect, exercisable by the Security Council authorizing military intervention as a last resort' (UN, 2004: para. 203). The UN reform summit that was then convened in September 2005 affirmed the 'responsibility to protect' in a specific form: It stated that all governments have the responsibility to protect their people from war crimes, genocide, ethnic cleansing and crimes against humanity. The international community has the responsibility to assist governments in living up to this responsibility. Only in the case that a country is manifestly unable or unwilling to do so does the responsibility to protect pass to the international community, which is represented by and acts through the UN Security Council. With a view to this resolution, it has been argued that today states have a 'responsibility to protect' that is on par with the right not to be interfered with (MacFarlane et al., 2004). Annan's successor, Secretary General Ban Ki-moon, has also pursued R2P with vigour. In January 2009, he issued a report on 'Implementing the Responsibility to Protect'. The report emphasizes the international collective responsibility to act to protect people within states while reaffirming the primary responsibility of the state and sovereignty and the need to build state capacity to that end.

However, because many countries of the South fear that the 'responsibility to protect' could serve as a pretext for unwarranted intervention, the international community remains split on the issue (Brock, 2009). Strong support comes from within the global North, including the EU, Canada, Japan, New Zealand, Australia and Norway, while some Arab states, Cuba, Iran, Pakistan, Venezuela and Vietnam have argued that R2P represents too great an intrusion into sovereignty. African states, while supportive of the principle, have voiced their concern that R2P might be misused in practice. Without coming to closure on these issues, in September 2009 the General Assembly adopted resolution 63/208, which takes note of the progress of the debate thus far and signifies the interest in continuing consideration of the principle of 'responsibility to protect'. When the Security Council in resolution 1973 decided in March 2011 to authorize the use of force in Libya, the resolution contained only general references to the 'responsibility to protect', despite the fact that the material content of the resolution was 'Protection of Civilians'.

The normative developments in the period since the end of the Cold War thus have had conflicting tendencies with respect to the issues of sovereignty and intervention. The

Security Council has developed the practice of regarding certain domestic events (like gross violations of human rights, or the breakdown of public order) as a threat to international peace. This has opened up the possibility of collective action pursuant to Chapter VII of the UN Charter. The assumption that sovereignty rests on a norm of unconditional non-intervention has been weakened, though it remains an open question as to whether R2P represents an emerging norm or only a concept yet to be specified. The Kosovo war and the war in Iraq have shown that intervention may take place regardless of any existing norms in international society. It is clear from the establishment of the Bush Doctrine and the willingness of the United Kingdom (as well as the other members of the 'coalition of the willing') to join the United States in its pre-emptive war that when major state leaders feel that war or intervention is in their interest, the normative foundation will not restrain their international actions. However, these normative foundations may increase the 'cost' of unilateral action by exposing governments to international moral outrage and other forms of critique which eventually may weaken their political support.

In practice, interventions in ongoing conflicts with serious violations of human rights remain *ad hoc* in their implementation. This is because of the uncertainty and risks which potential interveners face in dealing with domestic conflict. States will intervene only when and if they see the conditions as 'right'. But the criteria for what is 'right' do not necessarily reflect the needs of the countries in conflict. As a matter of rule, the interests of the potential intervener are decisive.

To be sure, there are fundamental changes that have taken place as a result of both the interventions that have occurred and the discussions surrounding R2P. The understanding of state sovereignty certainly is changing (Brunnee and Toope, 2004). But the analysis of these changes has been made difficult by the fact that there are still mutually inconsistent tendencies at work. Thomas Weiss argues that '[t]he notion that human beings matter more than sovereignty radiated brightly, albeit briefly, across the international political horizon of the 1990s' (Weiss, 2004: 135). For the United States and for most of the other major powers in the international system, the political will for humanitarian intervention waxes and wanes. The conclusion seems to be that sovereignty has taken on additional characteristics and become both a right and a responsibility. 'In brief, the three recognized characteristics of a sovereign state since the Peace of Westphalia (territory, authority, population) are supplemented by a fourth (respect for human rights)' (Weiss, 2004: 138). While a more consistent policy on protecting people in conflict may help to mitigate some of the human rights implications of fragile statehood and some steps in the development of a new normative framework have been taken in this direction, to the present this has not yet made a big difference in the practice of protecting people in conflict.

Moving Towards a More Complex Strategy

Granting former colonies legal independence and recognition of their sovereignty was accompanied by a normative obligation to provide development assistance to help substantiate the sovereignty claims of the post-colonial states with state building. In this sense, development assistance was a kind of intervention intended to build more capable states. The underlying hope was that economic, social and political development provided by both East and West would establish for these new states the means to gain substantial statehood. In short, fragile states would become well-functioning, capable states. The development assistance was in line with the modernization paradigm in development thinking (in both its Eastern and its Western version). The operating assumption was that all countries had at one point been traditional and backward and all countries could – and eventually would – become modern and advanced. While the East and West disagreed as to what a fully modern and advanced state would be, they shared the underlying assumptions of the modernization paradigm. Aid and foreign investment were seen as core facilitators of that process.

This aid was provided both bilaterally and multilaterally by countries and international organizations, and, in addition, thousands of non-governmental organizations (NGOs), supported by private charitable giving as well as governments, were created to assist fragile states. Thus, conterminously with the development of the norm of non-intervention in military terms, a practice of quite extensive international intervention for 'development' assistance emerged. The Second World War victors had established the Bretton Woods System (the World Bank and the IMF) to provide loans for rebuilding shattered entities after the war. A host of additional multilateral international organizational aid agencies channelled funds for development and provided the rules for their dispersal. Individual nations also provided bilateral assistance, distributing grants, loans and management assistance, often tied to quite specific national rules of procurement and dispersal. As they developed, NGOs brought their own principles and conditions for providing their funds and assistance as well.

Assistance and intervention may take many forms. For example, donors will often, as a condition of assistance, pressure states to conduct their affairs of state in a particular manner. They will link assistance to particular behaviours or policies, the simplest of which is requiring that aid is used to purchase the goods of the donor. Donors have also pressured recipient governments to accept aid projects that primarily benefited the donor rather than the recipient. While many of

these intervening forms of assistance may be invited or con-
sensual, they also often provide the recipient with little choice
but to approve the intervention or assistance. For much of
the forty years following the end of the Second World War,
the Cold War competition between the Soviet Union and the
United States dominated the approach of the two superpowers to development assistance as they sought to demonstrate
the superiority of their systems through their aid packages.
Such projects often took the form of very large demonstra-
tion projects chosen as much to 'wow' both international and
their own domestic audiences by their scope and scale as for
their long-term positive impact on the recipient. In addition,
aid assistance by the superpowers was heavily dominated in
terms of monetary value by military assistance and often took
the form of weapons and other war material and assistance in
the security sector. The important point is that in the context
of the Cold War, aid, on the one side, and socialist internationalism, or rather the idea of it, on the other, both helped
to keep up façades of viable statehood, shielding the respective countries from all too close scrutiny on the part of their
own populations or the international public. An indicator for
this may be seen in the way these states fared and development assistance shifted priorities after the end of the Cold
War. For example, as Raymond Copson has documented,
'US assistance to sub-Saharan Africa reached a peak in 1985,
when global competition with the Soviet Union was at a high
point. As the Cold War eased, security assistance programs
for Africa began to drop. Bilateral economic assistance for
Africa today remains close to the FY1990 low' (Copson, 2001:
1).

Thus the entire debate on failed, weak or fragile states
originated as the ideological blinders of the Cold War turned
obsolete. This is not to claim the utter uselessness of aid or
even its perniciousness, but it does point to the fact that East

and West were tempted to take the façade as reality because they believed in the superiority of their respective development models.

It is for this reason that development assistance from the very beginning was accompanied by a critical debate on its effects. This debate continues today (see, e.g., Collier, 2007; Easterly, 2006; and Moyo, 2009). There is little question that development assistance can help to improve food production, disease control, access to safe water and sanitation, infrastructure and the like (Sachs, 2006). But in as much as it stills amounts to intervention (i.e. a form of engagement which is limited in time and scope), it has only a limited influence on the way structure and process intersect in developing countries in general, and in fragile states in particular. Thus, in spite of the positive effects which development assistance may have and has had, it has only a minor impact on the overall combination of governments focused on coercion and clientelism; economies characterized by decline and lack of welfare; and civil societies driven by ethno-political and class rivalry.

During the Cold War years, East and West were not very much concerned about such shortcomings of their respective policies. They were more focused on gaining the loyalty of rulers and demonstrating their largesse than on the success of their aid assistance. Thus many aid recipients were not held accountable for their use of aid funds. Self-seeking elites could use aid to further their own economic and security interests and they soon learned that there was little threat that their aid would be reduced as a consequence. In addition, since a considerable portion of the aid provided to these nations was military and security-driven, it did little to help meet the needs of the populations of these countries.

Aid organizations and relief agencies were aware of the problems at an early stage. With the debt crisis of most weak states in the late 1970s, the World Bank began demanding radical reforms in weak states as a precondition for economic relief programmes (Callaghy, 1991; World Bank, 1994). There were also concomitant critiques arguing that this conditionality was a form of neo-colonialism, or, in the terms of Theresa Hayter (1971), that aid could be seen as a new form of imperialism. Critics further argued that development choices engineered by donors created dependence upon cash crops at the expense of subsistence farming. As a consequence, these fragile states were at the mercy of the vagaries of the international marketplace and their international trade became highly correlated with the patterns of assistance and nationalities of the donors and experts. As a result, there was often little improvement in the capacity of states to provide for their citizens. Many corrupt and non-democratic leaders were often dependent for their survival upon the aid that the superpowers and others were providing. Nonetheless, these same weak state leaders employed what Pierre Englebert (2009) has described as 'the power of sovereignty' to, in essence, hold the international community hostage to their corruption and mismanagement and thus ensure their continuation in power.

Much of this was to change at the end of the Cold War. With the ideological blinders of the previous years gone, elite behaviour moved centre stage as a good governance criterion emerged as one of the crucial requisites of successful development cooperation. At the same time, development cooperation was to become more conflict-sensitive. The latter implied three conditions: first, adhering to the principle of 'do no harm' which was at that time introduced by the NGO community (Anderson, 1999); secondly, making an active contribution to conflict resolution through non-military means (including the cooperation with NGOs in this issue area); and, thirdly, a systematic cooperation with military actors in the field (civil–military cooperation – CIMC), either within a multilateral framework (UN peace missions) or in the context of bilateral relations. In addition, development cooperation was to make greater efforts to increase its own effectiveness (OECD, 2005). This new approach included more systematic efforts at coming to grips with the notion of ownership and thus laid greater stress on putting the elites on the recipient end 'into the driver seat' of development cooperation, while – at the same time – these elites were to be urged to live up to the standards of good governance. Ideally, this would imply turning from the exertion of pressure to bargaining and to persuasion. In this way, the interventionist side of development cooperation could be played down and cooperation on equal terms played up.

In principle, increased conflict sensitivity of development assistance in combination with more social sensitivity on the part of the military (in the context of CIMC) and a stronger emphasis on controlling aid effectiveness opened up new prospects for coping constructively with fragile statehood. But in practice it has not made much of a difference yet. What has been gained in conceptual and normative terms so far may get lost in the context of the global power shift between the old West and the rising powers of the new East and its implications for the bargaining positions of the elites in fragile states, on the one hand, and the willingness of donor countries to subordinate their concerns about state fragility to their material and geo-strategic interests, on the other.

We turn now to our three cases. In previous chapters, we have explored how the Democratic Republic of the Congo, Afghanistan and Haiti have emerged as weak states and the conflict and violence that have beset them. In the next section we explore how external interventions in the past decade have impacted their situations.

The Democratic Republic of the Congo

As earlier chapters indicated, the trials and tribulations of the people of the state that is now known as the Democratic Republic of the Congo began long before their independence from Belgium in 1960. Since independence, the Congo has suffered long periods of both violence and predatory governance that have rendered one of the most resource-rich areas of Africa into a poor, weak and insecure state whose people have suffered greatly despite significant foreign assistance and military interventions over the past fifty years.

In the most recent period of this sorry history, in the context of the end of the 'Second Congolese War' in 1999, the United Nations Security Council created MONUC (the United Nations Mission in the Democratic Republic of the Congo – the acronym is from the French translation), a 20,000-troop peacekeeping mission, at that time the largest of the UN peacekeeping missions to monitor and mediate the peace process. Nonetheless, a 2008 study by the International Rescue Committee estimated a death toll of 5.4 million from 1998 to 2008, which, in addition to violent deaths, included deaths as a result of disease and starvation caused by the chaos of the conflict. On 28 May 2010, the United Nations Security Council (UNSC) adopted Resolution 1925, and transformed MONUC from a peacekeeping force to a 'stabilization mission' and renamed the mission the 'United Nations Organization Stabilization Mission in the Democratic Republic of the Congo' (MONUSCO). As of May 2011, there were 18,970 total uniformed personnel (16,896 military personnel, 729 military observers and 1,255 police), 978 international civilian personnel, 2,783 local civilian personnel and 607 UN volunteers who composed the MONUSCO mission.

The Congo well illustrates not only the international

community's attempts to make aid more strategic and its recipients more accountable, but also the continuing problems of achieving successful transformation in the process and bringing about the desired results. Despite adoption of the Country Assistance Framework (CAF) for the Democratic Republic of the Congo (DRC), a common strategic approach to recovery and development assistance (based on the Paris Declaration on Aid Effectiveness) which was agreed by a broad group of international partners, progress towards establishing a more effective, accountable and responsive state has remained minimal (Cahill, 2007).

Given the changes in the international community's approach, both economic and security support have been offered on the basis of the government of the DRC agreeing to democratic reform, particularly the holding of elections and promises of market liberalization. Joseph Kabila's administration also agreed to become a signatory of the Extractive Industries Transparency Initiative, designed to increase transparency in the mining sector and presumably both to reduce corruption and to encourage confidence in foreign investors (see Matti, 2010: 52). The international community pressed for democratic elections, but because of the widespread corruption (the DRC ranks 164th of the 180 nations in the Transparency International 2010 Corruption Perception Index), patronage and repression employed by the sitting Kabila government, the 2006 election was viewed by much of Congolese society 'from the highest Roman Catholic Church authorities and Congolese intellectuals to the vast bulk of the Congolese diaspora as a farce designed by the international community to legitimize the Kabila government' (Weiss, 2007: 141).

Stephanie Matti (2010: 53) further argues that, ironically, some of the success in pushing for democratic reforms and the increasing levels of foreign assistance has actually undermined democratic institutions. This occurs as capable

Congolese are drawn into aid administration from the public ministries because the salaries paid by donor projects are far in excess of those paid in the public sector and the aid undermines the establishment of a strong taxation system. This practice of ownership has had some unintended negative consequences within a society that can ill afford any additional problems.

At the same time, true to the tradition of the Congo's patrimonial and predatory government, Kabila replaced the heads of thirty-seven state enterprises with his own appointees, thus increasing his own economic power and political control. In the DRC, despite the intentions of the international community and the conditions for assistance, political positions and appointments continue to be seen as the source of personal and group economic benefits rather than as modes of building state and economic capacity. The high levels of corruption and the system that rewards political and ethnic supporters rather than merit continue to undermine the building of both state capacity and democratic and transparent institutions.

In this context, Melanie Roberts (2010) observes,

> the government thus far has been unable to institutionalize the rule of law. The continuing struggles in the Eastern Congo as well as general lawlessness in other parts of the country and widespread availability of weapons mean that the government lacks the monopoly of physical force, creating a situation in which various armed groups claim the loyalty of portions of the population.

The continuing lack of economic opportunity for the majority of the Congo's citizens, Roberts argues, feeds the security crisis, as ethnic and political cleavages become not only the basis for seeking opportunity but also the focus of hostility when such opportunities are not available, thus leading to further conflict and the continued undermining of the central government.

Clearly, the ongoing violent conflicts in the Eastern Congo have made progress extraordinarily difficult. However, there are also substantial underlying problems, discussed in chapter 3, that continue to plague the chances of improvement within the Congo. The international community, despite its ongoing presence and assistance, has been unable to alter the fundamental realities of the fragile Congolese state and to make up for its devastating impact on the historical legacy of the DRC.

Although one may argue that some progress has been made in some regions of the DRC over the past decade, continued instability in the north-east continues to threaten the viability of the state and the life chances of millions of Congolese citizens. All this continues despite heavy international involvement, the intention of which is to help put an end to the chaotic struggles. The Congo's warring factions continue to fight and, despite the existence of legal prohibitions and agreements, to engage in the despicable practices of utilizing child soldiers. The Congolese army (FARDC), the Congress for the Defense of the People (CNDP), the Democratic Forces for the Liberation of Rwanda (FDLR), the Nationalist and Integrationalist Front (FNI) and the Lord's Resistance Army (LRA) all recruit and maintain child soldiers. The young girls who are recruited not only are used as fighters but are often the victims of severe sexual abuse by their own side as well as their enemies. The future for these children, and by implication the DRC state and society, is clearly bleak and another generation may well be lost.

The prospects of effecting fundamental change from the outside are bleak. The first of these changes concerns the role of the Congo's immediate neighbours. As we saw in chapter 3, these neighbours were heavily involved in the wars and not necessarily simply as neutral observers who sought to reduce the fighting within the Congo because they feared that the conflict would spill over to their nations. Rwanda's Tutsis wanted retribution in the aftermath of the genocide there. Uganda hoped its intervention would aid the end of the civil war in its own northern territory by fighting the LRA in the Congo. The political regimes in Angola and Namibia sided with Kabila against the other neighbours to improve their own domestic standing.

Therefore, as we will argue in our general conclusion, the most important contribution of the international community to mitigating the present state of affairs appears to be a change in the international framework conditions. With regard to the DRC, new framework conditions include the enforcement of existing restrictions of the arms trade and a close monitoring of the transnational shadow economy that links up with regional conflict in the DRC. This would also call for a shift from 'ad hoc humanitarian approaches to a more comprehensive effort that addresses trade-offs inherent in the regional war economy' of the DRC (Gilpin and Funai, 2009: 1).

Afghanistan

Afghanistan is a pre-eminent case study of interventions in a fragile state. As we have shown in chapter 3, successive interventions from the British and the Soviet Union did not produce a state capable of effective national rule. The question is whether the present intervention by the United States and its NATO allies is doing, or will do, any better. The three successive long-term conflicts – the fight against the Soviets; the civil wars which resulted in the ascendancy of the Taliban; and finally the US-led NATO defeat of the Taliban along with the ongoing struggle of the Karzai government in Kabul to maintain its power and keep the 'deposed' Taliban at bay – have all taken a devastating toll on the population. Even though there is general agreement that there is no military solution to the conflict (Brahimi and Pickering 2011: 1), in the context of the current stage of the conflict, military considerations completely dominate the interests of the major intervening support powers, the United States and NATO. The 2009 report of the Agency Coordinating Body for Afghan Relief (ACBAR) has underlined the overall failure of development assistance in Afghanistan (Waldman, 2008). The assistance has not been effective in state building and has lacked sufficient funds for the task and national reach. Though there is some progress regarding education, the provision of healthcare and physical infrastructure, the security situation has deteriorated and the central state remains as fragile as it always has been.

The external attempts to create state capacity and an effective national state have all led to the frustration of the large majority of the population with the lack of development and effective reconstruction. Within Afghanistan, the Karzai government is widely considered corrupt. Non-Pashtuns feel that the government is favourable to the majority Pashtuns at the expense of the other tribal groups. The history of aid since 2001 has been that it has been directed primarily to military purposes, with military aid outweighing development aid by at least 15:1. Thus, a decade after the fall of the Taliban, Afghanistan has little to show in way of development, although Ashraf Ghani and Clare Lockhart (2008: 199–210) have argued that much has been put in place for development to eventually succeed. The Afghan government in Kabul and Afghanistan as a whole remains fully dependent on external assistance as nearly 90 per cent of public spending is supplied by foreign assistance (Waldman, 2008).

Development decisions have been almost exclusively limited to the elites in Kabul and the international donors. Ironically, given its own lack of capacity, until quite recently the central government, concerned that its own weakness would not allow it to compete with regional and local administrative political units, was not interested in strengthening government capacity at the subnational level and thus largely neglected this dimension. The result of this choice to ignore building subnational capacity served not only to continue to delegitimize the central government and denigrate its abilities for the majority of Afghans who live outside the capital, but also to strengthen the warlords and other competitors for power, such as the Taliban, who could at least deliver some services to populations in need. This is very much in line with the previous history of Afghan struggles between the centre and periphery discussed in chapter 3.

International donors, led by the United States and its NATO allies, have also imposed their own priorities. Counter-terrorism, counter-narcotics and counter-insurgency efforts have dominated their approach. Despite the recognition of the Paris Declaration on Aid Effectiveness (2005) with its emphasis on delivery and ownership, the cooperation of the Western donors with their Afghan partners has made little headway in putting an effective end to the insurgency, establishing a viable (and trusted) governmental security presence throughout the country, building up a much-needed infrastructure or improving the basic living conditions of the people.

Surveys which seek to gauge perceptions of the efficacy of the government and the Afghan people's trust in it consistently find that insecurity – attacks, violence and terrorism – is reported as the most important problem confronting the country. Such surveys find large majorities believing that the Afghan government fails to provide good governance, that local officials make money from drug trafficking, that government administrators in local areas are connected to the Taliban insurgency, and that, in general, foreign interference has worsened the security situation. These problems, plus the continuing corruption (Afghanistan ranks 176th in the Transparency International 2010 Corruption Perception

Index, tied for second most corrupt nation) and the external powers' dominant priority of counter-terrorism, have resulted in the inability to effectively transform the 'governing' practices of the regime.

These troubling survey results, coming almost a decade after the commencement of the overthrow of the Taliban, provide overwhelming evidence of the continued failure of the international attempts to enhance state capacity in Afghanistan. US administration officials still believe that security goals may be achieved and that their development assistance will ultimately provide long-lasting effects. However, these claims of progress, particularly in the context of the significant investment in lives and material, are consistently challenged as being driven primarily by American domestic political needs and consistently have proven to have been overly optimistic in their projections. The Fund for Peace Failed States Index, to which we referred in chapter 1 above, shows Afghanistan steadily increasing in fragility on most major dimensions. The country has risen from the eleventh most vulnerable nation in 2005 to the seventh in 2011 (Table 1.3, p. 23). While the causal linkages between the present state of affairs and international intervention require further discussion, there is little disagreement concerning the observation that the huge military input from the outside has been accompanied by a striking lack of success in coping with the country's basic predicaments.

Haiti

In contradistinction to the previous two cases discussed in this chapter, as we saw earlier, Haiti's situation as a weak state is not the result of a recent internal major war nor is its situation related to its recent emergence from colonialism. Nonetheless, prior to the devastating earthquake in Haiti in

January 2010, as Weiss (2007) has argued, despite years of substantial economic and political assistance, Haiti remained an impoverished, conflict-riven, violence-prone nation with a consistent record of gross human rights violations.

The aid that flowed into Haiti when Jean-Bertrand Aristide was re-installed as President in 1994 and in the aftermath of the civil-war-like situation during Aristide's second term (which resulted in his removal from Haiti) was not successful in changing the underlying political culture or in establishing a functioning and capable state. The international community's response to the constant struggles in the country did not effectively result in stabilizing Haiti or significantly improving the economic conditions of the Haitian people. Haiti at the beginning of 2010 remained a nation with severe pervasive poverty, a high level of crime, high rates of unemployment and significant shortcomings in infrastructure and public services.

MINUSTAH (the acronym of the French translation of the United Nations Stabilization Mission in Haiti) began operations on 1 June 2004 in the wake of the rebellion in January and February during the celebrations marking two hundred years of independence, which had led to the ouster of the Aristide government. MINUSTAH's mandate was firstly to ensure a secure and stable environment; secondly, to support a peaceful and constitutional political process; and, thirdly, to promote and protect human rights. Unlike most United Nations interventions, upon arriving in Haiti, the forces of MINUSTAH did not confront contending armies in the field. Rather, MINUSTAH and the host of other organizations within the international community that flowed into Haiti at this time confronted a state with serious organized crime networks, including gang violence and significant drug trafficking. Haiti was a society awash in unregistered weapons in the possession of armed groups. Further, its police force and judiciary appeared incapable of maintaining public safety and upholding the law. Because MINUSTAH was not created in the context of a war, it confronted a far more ambiguous situation of long-standing internal conflicts. There was no peace agreement or ceasefire among the contending forces (nor even one to help negotiate), nor were there official contending forces to confront.

After two years of MINUSTAH occupation, presidential elections, postponed four times and subject to many questionable 'standards', were finally held and René Préval, who had been Aristide's Prime Minister in his first government in 1990 and had himself been elected President in the democratic elections of 1996, secured enough votes to be declared the victor. Préval, who took office in May 2006, was unsuccessful in establishing his authority (or the state's) throughout the country. There was progress made, however, in the confrontation with the military that had dismissed Aristide (see Deibert, 2009). The international community provided substantial assistance to Haiti. However, four hurricanes in August and September 2008 ravaged the country and destroyed much of the previous aid efforts beyond the stabilization of the security forces.

MINUSTAH was unable to secure the confidence of the majority of the Haitian urban population because it was seen by a substantial number of Haitians as providing protection to the old political networks while failing to build up the institutions needed to support the rule of law and protect human rights. For the powerful elites, on the other hand, MINUSTAH and the international community were often seen as undermining the existing social and political structures, which had advantaged them at the expense of the political and economic participation of the rural population. Thus, while the peasants were hoping for change, elite groups sought the restoration of a strong political regime and security forces which could be employed to suppress the poor majority. MINUSTAH made little headway in addressing this basic divide within Haiti.

Then came the earthquake of January 2010. This destroyed not only the actual physical structures which housed the Haitian state, but also whatever minimal state capacity the government of Haiti had actually achieved after almost six years of UN intervention. Also destroyed in the earthquake were the Headquarters of MINUSTAH itself. In the words of UN Secretary General Ban Ki-moon, 'the earthquake has generated vast new needs and decimated the already weak capacity of the State to address them' (Haiti Innovation, 2010). In the immediate aftermath of the earthquake there literally was no Haitian government and MINUSTAH was required to replace it as the initial focal point for all the planning as well as logistical functions of the state to confront the resulting humanitarian crisis. Consequently, MINUSTAH, and particularly its military component, has assumed an even greater role within Haiti as it has had to begin literally reconstructing not only the institutions but also the actual physical locations to house the government and all the components of the Haitian state. The destruction extended to every aspect of Haitian life, from the distribution of food and water, to the construction of camps for displaced persons and the provision of security patrols to protect aid supplies as well as the population.

Thus in effect in post-earthquake Haiti, MINUSTAH was responsible for providing the core public goods (security, rule of law, infrastructure) and it, rather than the nonexistent government of Haiti, had to claim the monopoly of the legitimate use of physical force. At present, the Haitian state has regained minimal capacity to provide basic services, or to regulate and coordinate the myriad of non-state actors from the NGO community who are attempting to fill the large void that the earthquake has left in the country. The government's capacity, particularly in comparison to the scale of MINUSTAH and the international community, is still very limited and the slowness of its initial response to the earthquake coupled with the obvious discrepancy between its response and that of the external actors continues to forestall the development of trust in the Haitian government. In 2011, the presidential election saw renewed attempts by Aristide and even Jean-Claude Duvalier to return to Haiti and to re-enter politics. This dramatized the uncertainty over rule, governance and legitimacy in the country. More than two hundred years after independence, Haiti's core fragility problem thus remains: the almost nonexistence of the idea of a social contract between the Haitian state and its citizens. Instead politics in Haiti is structured around the basic antagonism between privileged elites who see government as the means to extract resources for their own purposes and to protect their dominant position in society, on the one hand, and the vast majority of the population who seek to gain effective access to, and support from, their government for the basics of security and society, on the other.

Conclusion

There are common themes that emerge from these three cases despite their differences in location, history and culture. All three states have been pressured by the international community to adopt the formal structures of democracy and all three have failed to institutionalize democracy beyond the formal holding of elections (and not all of these have been open and fair). The process and the outcome of elections have been less than exemplary for democratization. None of the three have emerged as democracies according to any neutral external observers. Patronage networks continue to dominate all forms of public policy and resource distributions and the three states continue to suffer from predatory public officials who see the state as the source of personal patronage networks rather than institutions for the public good. In all three of our cases, corruption is a major aspect of fragility. On the latest (2010) Transparency International Corruption Perception Index, Afghanistan is 179/180, Haiti 146/180 and the DRC 164/180. While corruption is not necessarily a cause of state weakness, as it exists in many stronger states, the corruption in these poor states is responsible for a much greater percentage of the state's economy than in stronger and wealthier states and is thus more pernicious in its effect.

In spite of massive international involvement in all three cases, violent conflict remains closely connected to the fragility of states and their inability to develop institutions of public safety, including a judiciary, that hold the trust of the population. In none of the countries has it proved possible to generate substantial change from outside intervention. On the one hand, this demonstrates the obstinacy of the problems of fragile statehood; on the other, it points to the limits of interventions, whether of a military or a non-military or a mixed nature. In Haiti, as in Kosovo in 1999, the international community has virtually taken over the state. This goes beyond intervention. It amounts not simply to the internationalization of rule (Schlichte, 2008), but rather to a complete internationalization of the state. However, this should be seen as an indicator more of the seriousness of the problems at hand than of the ability of the international community to 'fix' fragile states. After more than a decade of an intense international presence, Kosovo (and Bosnia, too, for that matter) would still be threatened by collapse if the international community left today. Again, this is not to say that outside involvement can never do any good in the context of state fragility. In serious emergencies, it may simply be indispensable. But in very fragile states, the internal structures and situations are not easily influenced from the outside and attempts to recast them in completely different moulds often fail. The goal of democracy promotion faces similar odds (Wolff and Wurm, 2011). The spread of democracy is highly desirable. But if democratization gets stuck half-way, it may serve as a pretext for combining old authority structures with new forms of violence-based social control.

There are strong limits to what outsiders can do in fragile states. They need to go home, sooner rather than later; recolonization is not on the agenda. They face limitations in terms of human and material resources, because domestic interests will be wary of foreign engagements. And they must be crucially dependent on the insiders who remain after the outsiders depart; they are the ones who must undertake and lead any sustainable project of state building and democratization. Fundamental social change must come from them, not from outsiders.

Violence accompanies the decline in trust within fragile societies. Outside engagement has had only limited success in building trust since it prevents 'normal' politics. International intervention may even forestall the development of trust not only for the respective national governments within the society, but also for the international community and its continued efforts to ease the fate of the people in conflict and to help overcome fragile statehood. As indicated, the agencies involved on the donor side are aware of these problems. We are then confronted with a dilemma. Intervention may seem to be the only way forward in cases where fragile states fail, and yet interventions themselves most often enhance fragility, prevent normal political developments and at best threaten and at worst destroy the trust and institution building required to address problems of fragility. Thus international society is in the unhappy position of 'damned if you do, and damned if you don't'. On the one hand, international society helped create fragile states through colonialism, the terms of decolonization in the context of the Cold War and its direct or indirect participation in the predatory practices of self-seeking elites. It did so in the context of the new norms of the United Nations (sovereignty and self-determination), which ensured the survival of both the new and the already existing weak states regardless of their actual capacity as states. On the other hand, international society now faces the dire consequences of fragile statehood. Fragile states cannot be subjected to permanent international trusteeship; but nor can international society stand idly by when state fragility turns into large-scale violence. Absent old patterns of war and conquest, there was no simple (even if not good) solution to weak political entities or statehood in the past, and as of today no simple solution to the problem of fragile statehood has yet emerged. The solution offered by the 'responsibility to protect' opens up conceptual space for dealing with some of the consequences of state fragility, but can it be developed as an effective practice?

CHAPTER FIVE

Surprising Deviations

Fragility Escaped

The special pathways to fragile statehood were portrayed in chapter 2. But history is never predetermined; some states that could have become fragile instead emerged as relative successes: they have more efficient governments based on the rule of law; their national economies are stronger and capable of sustained growth; and they have better developed national communities, in terms of both a 'community of citizens' and a 'community of sentiment'. How could this have happened when these states appeared to be set on the mainstream path of fragile statehood with weak governments, external domination and fragmented populations?

The development of capable government, a coherent economy and a fairly robust national community from an adverse starting point has been the exception in the global South. We examine two of these exceptions: Botswana in Southern Africa and Costa Rica in Central America. We explore how these two countries became relatively stable states at the same time that their neighbours and so many other states did not.

It should be noted at the outset that these countries are not flawless success stories: in each there is still poverty, inequality, hierarchy, cases of poor governance and, in the case of Botswana, a high level of HIV/AIDS. Still, they have been relatively successful and they are not prone to the violent conflicts that are the norm in many of the fragile states – the main problem with which we are concerned in this book. To put this in further perspective, it should be remembered that examples of all the problems mentioned above can also be found in the so-called 'advanced countries', including the United States, Western Europe and Japan.

So the puzzle remains: many other places in Africa and Latin America experienced a trajectory of increasingly fragile statehood. Colonial power was withdrawn without leaving strong administrative and institutional structures behind. Indeed, independent states were established on a weak and often incoherent foundation. Ethnic/regional/local bonds were often stronger than feelings of national community. In this regard, Botswana and Costa Rica also had a weak starting point. But they managed to overcome it despite the fact that most of their neighbours did not. Both of these countries avoided being drawn into the cycle of violence afflicting their regions. Both of them emerged as relative development 'successes', demonstrating that obstacles to development may be overcome. We will argue that central to the success of these two countries is the specific nature of the leadership and governance at critical moments in their political development (Acemoglu et al., 2003; Shafer, 1994). Furthermore, these countries had smaller and more concentrated populations and fewer ethnic divisions than many of the countries that have remained fragile. In this regard, they faced fewer challenges than most of the fragile states of today. But in absolute terms, the risk of failure remained high.

Botswana and Costa Rica represent cases where comparable historical and geographical preconditions in their regions led to different types of development outcomes, or, in other words, to situations where one country had success and neighbouring countries did not. Botswana is often seen as the African success story because it has fared well economically and politically compared with its neighbours. It is a landlocked and sparsely populated country and as such not a prime candidate for success. In other countries, a rich endowment of natural resources has turned into a 'resource curse'. It could have done so in Botswana. But it did not. Costa Rica's records on growth, development of political institutions and the building of nationhood testify to its exceptional status. Costa Rica, with its image of neutrality and strong political leadership, is referred to as a model and an example for the surrounding countries in the Central American region, though it, too, experienced various instances of domestic violence, which even escalated into a civil war in 1948.

The specific reasons for success are elusive. Indeed, we find fundamental disagreement in the literature over the relative importance of the main external and internal variables in providing explanations for success (Lange, 2009: 197). And there is not clear agreement in that literature on the theoretical background for explaining success. Some would even dispute that Botswana and Costa Rica are relevant cases. Ethnic divisions were comparatively less important here and the level of trust was higher than in other weak states. Comparative studies of success and failure work with few cases and each case can be argued to be 'special'. We focus on the elements commonly identified as the most salient in achieving success along the economic, political and social development dimensions. In particular, we look at these factors of state development through the historical lens of pre-colonial, colonial and post-colonial phases and we focus attention on the interplay between the external and the internal factors.

Botswana

At the time of independence in 1966, Botswana was one of the poorest countries in the world. Now it is a middle-income country with a GDP per capita higher than Bulgaria, Iran or Turkey. In the period of the past forty years it has one of the world's highest annual growth rates. It has a higher per capita income than neighbouring Namibia and South Africa and three times the income of neighbouring Zambia, not to mention Zimbabwe.

It has also been politically stable. It has had ten elections since independence, all of which external observers have characterized as free and fair. Botswana is the least corrupt country in Africa according to Transparency International and ranks thirty-third overall, ahead of many European nations. In terms of 'freedom of the press', it is ranked towards the top of the list in Africa. In the Fund for Peace Failed States Index for 2011 it ranks as country number 113. That makes it one of the best ranked countries on the African continent.

Pre-colonial Botswana consisted of a number of tribal societies that became highly stratified with distinct systems of hierarchy during the nineteenth century. It was comprised of both wetlands and desert, and farming relied heavily on cattle herds. Tribal chiefs controlled the land and others were obligated to provide the chief with a tribute in the form of milk and meat. This created large income differences. There was individual ownership of cattle, but many chiefs had amassed large herds of cattle. One chief is reported to have had a herd of 8,000 head of cattle by 1880 (Good, 1992: 70).

Studies of the tribal structures in early Botswana have made a point of highlighting the role of *Kgtola*, a system of village meetings or tribal gatherings where all men could meet, all could speak and consensus was stressed as the means for making decisions. The power of the chief and the dominant cattle owners formed the backbone of the political structure, and the system was accessible and responsive. Consensus was shaped by both interdependence and patronage. Strong central authority was combined with strong local representation; 'a chief is a chief through the people', according to a Tswana saying (Pitcher et al., 2009: 146). Pre-colonial state organization was based on a system of tribute collection and cattle production. A weak political system of control and continuity was in existence before colonial times, with some elements of national governance. A system of regional 'governors' was established and 'boundary watchmen' were appointed. Cattle trading posts were tied to the 'king'.

Pre-colonial institutions were preserved in both colonial and post-colonial times. This is important for success because large-scale disruptions of institutions vastly increase the risk of neo-patrimonialism: that is, self-seeking elites using state resources to secure support. Creating new institutions provides for increased pay-off possibilities to client networks; Botswana avoided that (Lange, 2009). The colonial period in Botswana lasted from 1885 to 1966. The specific course it took makes up an important part of the development success story of Botswana today. Already in 1870, Batswana chiefs had asked for British protection because Dutch and German settlers encroached on their lands from their bases in South Africa and Namibia. The British protectorate of Bechuanaland was set up as an answer to these requests. It served to secure strategic British interests, but also to prevent the territory from being annexed by Dutch and German colonialists. Achieving protection from external threats was a primary concern for the Batswana chiefs, who agreed to accept British power, but from the beginning they nonetheless resisted any widespread and close British rule.

Great Britain's benign neglect has been identified as one of the reasons for the relative success of political and social development in the country, because the inclusive pre-colonial institutions were not destroyed (Acemoglu et al., 2003). The *Kgtola* encouraged a system of balance and equality among the tribes, resulting in less conflict. This system was continued during colonialism. Furthermore, Great Britain took little away from Botswana in terms of resources and imposed little on the country except religion, defined laws of private property and the rule of law. During the independence period, Botswana also achieved a few important reforms of the pre-existent power structures (Lange, 2009: 197).

This is not to say that Great Britain did not in fact have an impact. It did. The so-called 'hut tax' introduced in 1899 forced a great number of men from Botswana to work in the mines in South Africa. This mass migration of labour (in 1943 it was estimated to be nearly 50 per cent of the adult male population) had a significant effect on the social and economic fabric of society (Beulier, 2003: 233) because it served to strengthen the cattle elite, and enabled the continued development of a cattle-based economy (Good, 1992: 72). The political system of the colonial period was built on affinities of interest between the colonial administrators and the traditional chiefs. The few colonial investments, such as the establishment of water wells, provided for better and larger grazing areas in the first half of the twentieth century and further strengthened the importance of local chiefs.

One analysis argues that Britain's failed attempts to incorporate Botswana in the South African Union produced an impetus towards nation building in the country, because it made the elite interested in the creation of a national community (Lange, 2009: 146). This interest was strengthened by the effects of the governing crises spurred in 1948 by the exiling of Seretse Khama, chief of the Bamangwato tribe. During his education in Britain, he had married a white woman, and since he was an important leader, South Africa threatened reprisals against Botswana if this violation of apartheid was accepted. Internal non-cooperation and conflict resulted from the banning of Seretse. The British were thus forced to institute a form of direct rule from 1954 to 1966 in Botswana. In this context, ironically by creating a civil service based on meritocracy, the British strengthened the institutions and bureaucracy of the soon to be independent state (Lange, 2009:

140). Overall, colonialism thus strengthened existing structures. The disruption at independence was brief and resulted in effective reform.

Decolonization itself was a brief and relatively smooth process, particularly when compared to many other African states, such as the Democratic Republic of the Congo. The party that dominates Botswana even today (the BDP, Botswana Democratic Party) was dominant from its inception in 1961. It was founded by Seretse Khama, who had returned from exile in 1954. Helped into power by the colonial administration and with financial support from both the domestic and international ranching community, the party took control of the state at independence in 1966. Seretse Khama's political decisions made at the time of independence, such as the transfer of mineral property rights from the tribes to the state (discussed below), combined with the support of both the colonial administration and the relatively wealthy ranching communities were very important in setting Botswana on a pathway away from state fragility. These examples underscore the importance of the specific nature of the leadership and the governance structures around that leadership in the development of state capacity.

Botswana's development path over the last almost fifty years has followed the paths laid out in the preceding periods. Politically, the BDP has been in power for the entire period and has managed to win every election in a predominately free and fair manner. Though support for the party has declined, it still received 53 per cent of the vote in the 2009 election. The current President, Ian Khama, is the son of Botswana's first President, Seretse Khama, and the great grandson of Botswana's pre-colonial king Khama III. This democratic stability distinguishes Botswana from all but a few African countries.

We are not arguing that all is perfect. Botswana's democracy has not been tested with a democratic changeover of government in the post-colonial period, and there are instances of power abuses. Some argue that underneath the democratic front there is an autocratic system of ruling party dominance and presidentialism (Good, 2008: 70). However, most analysts claim that the level of abuse of legal command and authority which is common in many African countries is not the rule in Botswana. The civil service, the political system and the political culture manifest a degree of responsiveness and accountability that have proven important in unlocking Botswana's development path (Englebert, 2009: 221). Botswana had an average annual rate of economic growth of 9 per cent in the forty years after independence. This makes the country one of the few nations in the world to have had sustained economic growth for a long period of time (World Bank, 2009: 2).

Botswana's economic progress was greatly aided by the development of diamond mines. The continuous and stable generation of surplus created by the mines has had a powerful impact on the wealth of the country. One-sided dependency on mineral wealth frequently poses severe risk for weak states (cf. the Democratic Republic of the Congo, DRC). Botswana, however, managed to avoid the resource pitfall of other mineral-rich/ diamond countries. The decision by the first post-independence premier, Seretse Khama, to transfer mineral property rights away from his own Bangwato tribe to the government (and thus to the state as a whole) contributed greatly to political stability. In countries like the DRC or Sierra Leone, the wealth of the mines became a factor in blocking development because of conflict and war over the control of the income. In Botswana, the huge diamond discoveries in 1968 and in 1976 led to an agreement with De Beers, the large South African mining company. Both politically and economically, this agreement created stability instead of turning into a 'resource curse' because of some unique circumstances. Politically, the choice was made to have the income flow to the Botswana state. Economically, on the one hand, De Beers was under pressure in South Africa and therefore interested in a stable arrangement in Botswana; on the other hand, the discovery of new, attractive deposits increased the bargaining power of Botswana (Easterly, 2006: 360). Diamond production today accounts for more than 40 per cent of GDP.

The wealth generation from diamonds provided a surplus in the political system that furthered the interests of members of all three Botswana tribes in the smooth functioning of the state. Subsequent government investments in health and education and improvement of infrastructure created a welfare system unusual in the region (World Bank, 2009). The continued stable political leadership and its investment and property policies are credited with a large part of the reason why Botswana became a success. Leadership and decent governance have made a big difference in Botswana (Beulier, 2003: 235).

As indicated above, there is a dark side to the economic success. According to World Bank estimates, a third of the people of Botswana have been left behind. Rural poverty, HIV/AIDS and income inequality are significant problems. Botswana's income inequality is the fifth worst in the world (World Bank, 2009). The country is also unable to generate sufficient employment and the unemployment rate hovers around 20 per cent. The country's narrow economic base presents significant challenges for further development.

With such glaring economic and social inequalities, does Botswana have a coherent national community? Are legal, political and social rights provided to such an extent that citizenship and national community building is fostered? Botswana's story is one of remarkable consistency in loyalty to the country and its institutions. One of the mechanisms has been to create a positive feedback between the governmental provision of welfare goods and the ensuing support for the state. Voting in Botswana has been consistently high with participation rates of over 70 per cent. Although there are human rights abuses, both the US State Department and Amnesty International reports list only a few violations.

Despite wars and violent conflict during pre-colonial and colonial times, Botswana has seen little violent conflict since independence. This is because of the consultative character of pre-colonial Botswana, the consolidation of democratic institutions and the growth of an educated urban population. This has helped create both citizenship and national community. The growth of a vibrant civil society in the country, however, is more recent and still weak. This is based on a close interplay between an active NGO sector and a political system that is now more determined to include it in policy making (Caroll and Caroll, 2004: 341). Equality of women has become a particular issue of emphasis in Botswana. The paternalistic – we take care of them – political culture was based on scepticism towards an active growth of civil society. Beginning with the growth of the women's movement and reinforced by internal and external pressures on the country, this attitude started changing about the time of the 1994 election (Caroll and Caroll, 2004: 349).

In sum, what is it that accounts for Botswana's relative success? First, the early historical experience must be emphasized: pre-colonial state organization was both robust and responsive. Later on, the leadership used this strength intelligently to create a capacity for effective intervention, politically, economically and socially. Botswana is a somewhat homogeneous, small country where skilful political leaders have been interested in providing the services of a functioning state to its citizens. The leadership saw self-interest and the society's interest as overlapping, and those in power were perceived by potential contenders as legitimate power holders. As a result, self-seeking elites did not come to dominate Botswana. As we have seen in the cases of the Democratic Republic of the Congo, Afghanistan and Haiti, fragility grows when government is illegitimate and not based on the rule of law. Building from existing tribal structures, Botswana created lawful government.

The availability of an economic surplus in the hands of the elite meant that the state had something to offer the stakeholders. Furthermore, diamond mining created a possibility to pursue a combination of capitalist development with a relatively strong, interventionist state (Good, 1992: 94). Success was created through 'strong leadership that adopted good policies and built the institutions needed to develop those policies' (World Bank, 2009: 2). In combination with this, the discipline and the vision of a small technocratic/bureaucratic class has been one of the remarkable elements of the success (van de Walle, 2004: 7).

The second development that accounts for Botswana's success is that the country escaped the most invasive impositions by the colonial powers, in spite of the fact that Britain did have designs to incorporate the country in either Cecil Rhodes's company or the South African Union (Lange, 2009). It also escaped the most invasive meddling after independence by organizations such as the IMF and the World Bank because it had resources of its own. In short, it avoided heavy external domination. The colonial legacy of creating Botswana as a 'peaceful' protectorate protected the country from incursions and encroachments. This gave the country a better starting point than neighbouring Namibia. Being a front-line state facing the apartheid regime in South Africa generated favourable Western aid in the 1970s and 1980s. The international reputation of a development darling, a 'success story', reinforced the success both externally and internally (van de Walle, 2004).

Costa Rica

Costa Rica is high on indicators of human development, government effectiveness and GDP growth. The high score is particularly noticeable in the areas of political indicators (government effectiveness, rule of law, voice and accountability and freedom) and in the 'security' area, where a high score means absence of conflict, absence of human rights abuses, political stability and the absence of violence. On the 2011 Fund for Peace Foreign Policy Index of Failed States, Costa Rica ranks 137th. On these sets of indicators, Costa Rica does better than most Latin American countries and much better than the neighbouring Central American countries of Panama, Honduras, Nicaragua and Guatemala. Neighbouring Nicaragua exhibits much lower scores on governmental effectiveness, rule of law and control of corruption and ranks 67th on the 2011 Fund for Peace Failed States Index. On social welfare indicators, Costa Rica does better, too. The World Bank labels Costa Rica a development success because of its steady economic expansion over the past thirty years and points to the country's strategy of outward-oriented export-led growth as the key to the high level of foreign investments in the country and its rapid GDP growth.

On measures of poverty and inequality, the country also performs better than the Latin American average. The country has less poverty than Panama, the neighbour to the south with a similar GDP per capita, and with similar high recent growth rates (Economist Intelligence Unit, 2008: 22). According to the UNDP Human Poverty Index, where a high ranking means low poverty, Costa Rica ranks 11th whereas Panama ranks 30th; Nicaragua ranks 68th (UNDP, 2009).

How did Costa Rica arrive at this relatively high position? As we shall see, a central factor for Costa Rica's success, as in the case of Botswana, has been the role of the leadership and governance at critical moments in its political development. In addition, as was the case with Botswana, the country had fewer ethnic divisions and a somewhat less fragile starting point than some of its neighbours.

When Columbus reached the North American mainland on his fourth expedition in 1502, he eventually landed on the coast of what is now Costa Rica, but no colony was established. In pre-colonial times, there were distinct cultural regions in the area. The eastern part was influenced by the Mayan culture, but had small chieftainships and was politically fragmented. This was very different from the high level of organization of the native groups to the north. In the south-western part, the population was dispersed and influenced by the culture from the northern part of South America. In cultural terms, the country was thus a mixed boundary area between the Meso-American civilization to the north and the Andean civilization to the south.

Spanish colonization in the region proceeded slowly. Its main centre was in Guatemala and only a small number of Spaniards settled in Costa Rica; it was considered a periphery. However, the settlement that did take place had disastrous consequences for the local population. The Native American population was, over a period of one hundred years, reduced to virtually nothing. Disease, war, relocation and exploitation did away with most of the native inhabitants. It has been estimated that of the original population in 1500 of 400,000 people there were fewer than 10,000 in 1610 (Palmer and Molina, 2004: 10).

This scarcity of indigenous people and manpower resulted in a different pattern of colonization. The rigid hierarchies associated with Spanish colonial rule were of less importance here. In the Central Valley of the country, a society of small and medium-sized farms gave birth to a society of peasants and merchants. Though far from equal or even remotely democratic, the society was less hierarchical and had fewer ethnic divisions than the neighbouring Central American countries (Cardoso, 1991: 43). Despite its name (Costa Rica: The Rich Coast), there were no major resources to extract and there was a shortage of indigenous labour needed for running large-scale farms. The result was that a small-farmer, largely self-sufficient economy was built during the colonial period. Many of the farmers worked the land themselves.

The colonial period took its distinct flavour from the peripheral nature of Costa Rica. Guatemala was the centre and Costa Rica the periphery. Because of the distance to the regional centre, colonial institutions here were given more local influence; Costa Rica was not considered important. National integration also took a different course. Because of race mixes and the few remaining Native Americans, social hierarchies were built on wealth rather than on ethnic background, and initial differences in wealth were not that large. This distinguished the country's integration from that of most other Latin American countries (Cruz, 2005: 67).

The population was concentrated in the Central Valley, where four-fifths of the approximately 60,000 population (1824) lived and worked. This created closer social integration than in countries where the populations were more dispersed (Robinson, 2008: 179). Finally, conflicts in society were from early on channelled more along institutional and legal lines than elsewhere, because of the relative homogeneity of society. In sum, because of its peripheral status in colonial times, Costa Rica avoided a large degree of external domination, and because of the relatively egalitarian society, social divisions and hierarchies did not run deep. But it was utterly poor. A colonial Spanish governor called Costa Rica 'the poorest and most miserable colony in all America' (Shafer, 1994: 185).

Independence came early to Costa Rica as it did to all of Latin America in comparison with the rest of the global South.

After the 1821 declaration of independence, followed by a civil war in 1823 and the short-lived Federal Republic of Central America, Costa Rica became fully independent in 1838. In what turned out to be a crucial decision, coffee was chosen after independence as a source of income and export earnings. Coffee could be grown on smaller lots and in a dispersed manner. Free seedlings and land were distributed to promote coffee production and it worked well. In the 1850s, there were 3,000 hectares of coffee. Forty years later, this had expanded to 14,000 hectares; exports of coffee generated 80 per cent of export earnings (Shafer, 1994: 185).

Surplus from coffee and later banana production made possible a much-needed expansion of infrastructure. It also paved the way for rising imports. Thus, the wealth from coffee had impacts everywhere: the modernization of coffee production itself, the expansion of trade and services and a stimulation of urbanization (Seligson, 1980: 17–22). At the same time, land ownership became increasingly concentrated and a large number of smallholders became landless labourers.

During the nineteenth and early twentieth centuries, politics in Costa Rica was an elite affair, involving little more than 10 per cent of the citizenry (some of what follows draws on Sørensen, 1991: 147–9). Power was firmly in the hand of the coffee aristocracy. However, the nature of elite rule was markedly different from that of most other countries in Latin America. Costa Rica did not have a semi-feudalistic hacienda system with Indians and slaves under the control of a rural elite; the rural working class was free of extra-economic coercion and there was an independent peasantry.

Even if the coffee barons exploited their political supremacy for the benefit of their own economic interests, they were imbued with liberal values of religious freedom, freedom of the press and the promotion of public education. A law had already passed in 1884 which established free, compulsory, secular education (Ameringer, 1982: 19). Democracy was being built. The election of 1909 was the first in which an increasingly active opposition successfully appealed to strata of the population outside the aristocracy. And civil society was also in the making. The Communist Party was an efficient organizer of banana workers during the depression of the 1930s, and many other groups were organized as well.

It is true that an 'agrarian-commercial capitalist class' (Peeler, 1985: 61) dominated the Costa Rican scene until 1949, but there were increasing challenges from several other groups, created by the forces of education and organization. With the election of Rafael Angel Calderón Guardia as President in 1940, Costa Rica had for the first time a national political leader who responded to the demands from popular forces which had expressed themselves in domestic unrest following the loss of export markets in the wake of the First World War and the world economic crisis of 1929. While not attempting profound changes of the social structure, Calderón did seek to provide tangible benefits to workers and poor people (Peeler, 1985: 67). The most important results of these efforts were a social security system and a labour code.

Calderón refused to acknowledge defeat in the 1948 presidential election. He was challenged by an armed uprising led by José Figueres Ferrer, founder of the Social Democratic Party. After six weeks of fighting, the government surrendered, and in the transition period which followed, the basis for ensuing decades of democratic rule in Costa Rica was formed (Peeler, 1985: 66–76). The social democratic forces who toppled Calderón continued the welfare-orientated policies he had initiated. The constitution of 1949 extended the franchise to women and created an obligation to vote for every citizen over eighteen years of age. The armed forces were abolished and the banks were nationalized. The constitution also created the powerful Tribunal Supremo de Elecciones, an independent organ whose purpose is to oversee all aspects of the electoral process and whose members are appointed by the Supreme Court. The Tribunal has helped to remove almost all of the incidences of fraud in Costa Rican elections. It should be added that the Communist Party was constitutionally prohibited until 1970 (the movement was tolerated under another name). Another restriction on democracy was the literacy requirement for voting (mitigated by a high literacy rate at an early stage).

By 1949, then, a liberal democratic structure had been formed in which the rural elite of agro-exporters had to share political influence with urban middle sectors and some popular groups. In the following decades, this broad 'coalition' grew stronger through its control of the state apparatus and new social groups were incorporated into the alliance. Political power has been held by the main factions of this coalition in the way that they have alternated in occupying the presidency. Their common ground has been a commitment to economic and social modernization with an expanded role for the state. This delicate balance between forces of the status quo and forces of change is an important factor for understanding the Costa Rican trajectory of development.

Sharply rising interest rates increased the burden of Costa Rica's external debt in the 1980s. The state had to accept IMF austerity measures in order to secure financial stability. Finding the appropriate balance between private sector growth sufficient to secure the necessary resources and public welfare aimed at equity and poverty alleviation continues to be a major challenge in Costa Rica. The presence of 500,000 Nicaraguan immigrants, who came during the 1980s civil war in Nicaragua, in a country of 4.5 million people is another great challenge. At the same time, Costa Rica has attracted considerable foreign investment from the United States, and is considered an attractive retirement destination for North Americans.

In sum, what explains Costa Rica's success? First, the early historical experience was different from most other areas of Spanish settlement. It had less hierarchy and fewer ethnic divisions; the basic unit in the country was the self-sufficient, independent farmer working his homestead. The introduction of coffee as an export commodity in the period right after independence combined with the absence of strong rent-seeking groups laid a foundation of overall economic growth that has served as a basis for social development. In the nineteenth century, the liberal coffee barons introduced public education and freedom of the press. The political system was not democratic from the beginning, but it was responsive to organized public pressure at a quite early stage. The constitution of 1949 created a solid basis for liberal democracy in a shared commitment between elites, middle sectors and popular groups. Thus political leadership and governance at critical moments in Costa Rica's history chose to accommodate the demands of key groups in society and thereby set the country on a different trajectory from other Central American states.

Second, Costa Rica was never seriously dominated by outsiders. It was simply too poor to be of considerable interest to the Spanish Crown; later on, it was considered an island of liberal democratic stability in an otherwise unruly region and was never targeted for hostile intervention by the United States.

Conclusion: Factors Enhancing Stable Statehood

Three major elements help us understand the relative success of Botswana and Costa Rica. The first element reaches deep into pre-colonial (Botswana) and early colonial (Costa Rica) history: the absence of purely self-seeking elites combined with relatively effective leadership and responsive government at an early point. Fragile states, in contrast, have self-seeking elites set on their own short-term maximization of power and profit rather than on general development. In Costa Rica, relative poverty and lack of social hierarchy prevented the emergence of any elite for a long period. When it did emerge with the coffee barons, it was less entrenched and more ready to combine self-interest with the pursuit of general development. In Botswana, the early *Kgtola* system helped create a balance of interest among the tribes. It also laid the foundation for an open and accountable political culture. In both countries, the search for a workable consensus on development was made easier by the homogeneous nature of their social structures. Small and relatively concentrated as the populations were, social cohesion became easier to achieve and build on than was the case in large states with a diverse and scattered population base. At key moments in the development of both countries, leading elites emerged who chose policies that strengthened state building rather than the short-term interests of the elite in power. It is important to stress that, had this not been the case, Botswana and Costa Rica could easily have headed down the same destructive paths that we witnessed in Haiti and the Democratic Republic of the Congo, with all the attendant difficulties of reversing course.

The second element is also relevant for a long historical period. It concerns the fact that Costa Rica and Botswana were spared intense external domination. Both countries had a peripheral status in the colonial period so that external domination had less adverse effects than in many other countries. In Botswana, the British interest was in making sure that other states did not come to control the country; the British were thus content to extend a security umbrella over the country and not seriously intervene in many other ways. In Costa Rica, the Spanish colonization had its focus on Guatemala. Costa Rica was considered a poor and uninteresting region and played a marginal role in the Spanish colonial system. The two countries had a better starting point than many in terms of building state strength. This enabled a wider agenda of possibilities for the political leadership in the two countries.

The third element, success breeds success, might at first glance appear tautological, but that is not necessarily the case. Once a relatively effective political and economic system is in place, once a society has been formed with a great deal of cohesion and moderate amounts of social tension, then the country is better positioned to reap additional benefits and to exploit the opportunities for further development that might come into view. For example, such favourable societal structures increase the likelihood that emerging political leaders will be more effective, less self-seeking and more bent on general political, economic and social improvement. Botswana and Costa Rica have indeed been blessed with a series of 'good' leaders in this respect, not merely because they were lucky, but because societal structures were in place that supported the emergence of 'good' leaders.

In the economic realm, Botswana was indeed lucky to discover rich diamond deposits, but in many other countries diamonds have been a curse rather than a blessing (recall the 'blood diamonds' in Sierra Leone and the 'resource curse' in many other countries). In Botswana, an effective state exploited the diamonds to the benefit of general development of the country. In Costa Rica, conditions for coffee farming were excellent; but excellent conditions for coffee farming exist in other countries (e.g. Kenya and Ethiopia) that have not been able to reap similar benefits from that fortunate situation. Again, societal structures in Costa Rica were decisive for the successful outcome.

We emphasized in the opening of this chapter that history is not predetermined; some potentially fragile states have been success stories. The two cases demonstrate the peculiar and extraordinary circumstances that were in play to create this result. Botswana and Costa Rica avoided being dragged into a negative cycle of violence, state failure and outside intervention. As we have seen in chapter 3, the mainstream path creating violence in fragile states is linked to the fact that these states are 'limited' in their capacity, have self-seeking elites and are unable to pursue state-building reform. Botswana and Costa Rica escaped this. Fighting over the economic spoils of the state has led to violence and fragility elsewhere. In Botswana and Costa Rica, the economic gains were used for state building, in terms of state capacity both to govern and to distribute economic and social goods. Finally the role of outsiders, as we saw in chapter 4, has been benign in the case of these two countries, where no foreign interventions have taken place and where outside interference has been less disruptive and reasonably well managed. In contrast, in the cases of the Democratic Republic of the Congo, Afghanistan and Haiti, outside interventions further eroded state authority and legitimacy.

Conclusion
The Fragile State Dilemma

Fragile Statehood: Structure and Process

As an ideal type of state, fragile states are characterized by serious deficiencies in three areas: government, economy and nationhood. They emerged from a process of state formation which is qualitatively different from the trajectories of the modern states in Europe, North America and elsewhere. They are fragile entities mainly as a result of the power of self-seeking elites in combination with a history of external domination. Most fragile states came about because colonialism was no longer acceptable. They survive because the international community has been willing to accept their claims to sovereignty.

Sovereignty is a vital source of power and influence for the ruling elite in fragile states; for ordinary people in these states, by contrast, sovereignty often has been a source of insecurity. In these states, self-seeking state elites have 'captured' the state apparatus to their own advantage. Typically, the state is treated as the property of a leading strongman and his select group of clients. The majority of the population is excluded from the system and faces a state that is more an enemy and a threat than a protector and a champion of development. Thus, while the elites in fragile states may be afraid of a strong security sector themselves (because it may become a source of strong opposition), state fragility does not mean that the state lacks the means to oppress its people.

This, then, is the general background for the fundamental predicament of fragile states. It emerges from the paradoxical situation that fragile states are free from external threats to their territorial integrity while simultaneously the fragile state itself poses a serious security threat to major parts of its own population. In a basic sense, the notion of international anarchy and state order appears to be turned around: there is an international system of relative order with fairly secure protection of the borders and territories of fragile states, and there is a domestic realm with a high degree of insecurity and conflict.

Fragile statehood is violence-prone. We have clarified the links between fragile statehood and violence, both in general terms and in concrete cases. First, there is a self-help element: incumbent elites use violence in order to remain in power and to fight off challengers; contenders for state power use violence as well. Ironically, both sides may have an interest in a weak security sector: ruling elites fear they will be challenged by new rivals should the security sector grow strong; common people fear that a strong police and military sector will result in more repression rather than less. That perpetuates a situation of violence-prone insecurity.

Second, economic interests and social factors are involved: those in power want to siphon off economic resources for their own benefit; contenders seek to get their share of what is available. Both are ready to use violence to pursue their interests. Ethnic and religious identities come into play as an amplifier in confrontations between groups. Differences in ethnic/religious identities thus make violent confrontations between groups more brutal and relentless when they are mobilized as part of the conflict; yet they are rarely themselves the root cause of conflict. This also holds true for the economic interests that come to bear in violent struggles. Thus, while economic interests feed into such struggles, their root causes are political rather than economic.

Finally, outsiders have had major responsibility for the high level of conflict in fragile states. Colonial rulers were often violent in the extreme; after independence, outsiders would support rulers and regimes in fragile states to gain support for their side in the Cold War. More domestic violence was often the result. At the same time, the high level of violence by domestic groups depends both on their outside connections being willing to deliver arms, supplies and the means of communication to coordinate military actions, and on the demands for the goods (including drugs, diamonds and strategic raw materials) that insiders have to offer. This situation persists and may even be aggravated as part of the 'war on terror' and the struggle for strategically important resources.

The Role of International Society

Since decolonization and especially since the end of the Cold War, the attitudes towards formal, sovereign statehood have begun to change. International society still accepts the principle of self-determination, but this acceptance is no longer based on the disregard of the domestic conditions within states. International society increasingly intervenes in fragile states in order to promote substantial state building. This intervention can be interpreted as an attempt by international society to assume responsibility not merely for the formal persistence of states, but also for the development of effective government in these countries. However, international society is not well prepared or even suited to carry out this task successfully. There are both external and internal impediments, as we have seen.

First of all, there is a normative dilemma: the norm of non-intervention upholding all sovereign governments, including the fragile ones, exists alongside an emerging international norm which maintains that grossly ineffective government is unacceptable. According to the first norm, intervention is considered a violation of international law; according to the second, outside intervention is claimed to be mandated especially in conflicts in which governments are not able or willing to protect the people from genocide, war crimes, ethnic cleansing and crimes against humanity (the 'responsibility to protect').

Second, there is a substantial dilemma: international society is not willing to accept full responsibility for the creation of strong and viable states; perhaps even more problematic, there is no evidence as yet that international society has the capacity (within any meaningful time frame) to make fragile states strong, viable and capable of serving their populations. The resulting hesitant engagement is fraught with problems. As we have seen in the unhappy cases of the Democratic Republic of the Congo, Afghanistan and Haiti, even decades-long, expensive interventions may not lead to stronger and more viable states and may at times do even more harm than good.

Perhaps the most serious problem is that the norm of sovereignty continues to place bargaining power into the hands of local elites interested in exploiting any resources available at the expense of the nation as a whole. Some have suggested that the international community should take responsibility in these cases (Krasner, 2009: 232), but an across-the-board policy of international trusteeship is neither feasible or desirable, nor legally acceptable. For these reasons, fragile states persist, even in the face of many new initiatives by the international community to do something about this by intervening in an ongoing conflict and/or by engaging in peace building and state building in post-conflict situations. Unfortunately, strategies of both intervention and non-intervention are problematic. Non-intervention simply means leaving self-seeking elites alone, as evidenced by the examples of Mugabe in

Zimbabwe or the military junta in Myanmar. Interventions, on the other hand, develop a dynamic of their own, making it difficult to confine it to limited purposes.

Beyond immediate political stabilization, or disaster relief, attempts at democratization and the creation of a stable security environment involve long-term commitments. They only have a chance of success with corresponding local commitment, participation and ownership. Given the conditions under which interventions have been generated, these are not easily produced. The reason behind this difficulty is that fragile states are not necessarily characterized by total anarchy. Rather, a lack of bureaucratic authority (in the Weberian sense) may at least in part be compensated by complex ways of negotiating statehood between the centre, the regions and the local communities. Outsiders are usually not in a position to link up with such complex ways of producing authority and may destroy whatever statehood there is in fragile states instead of advancing state building (Hagmann and Hoehne, 2009).

The cases of relative success that we have visited present a mixed picture as regards overcoming fragile statehood with the help of outsiders. On the one hand, Botswana and Costa Rica developed differently because of peculiar circumstances related to their early histories and because they were relatively free from external domination. Self-seeking elites were tempered by countervailing forces or did not even emerge.

On the other hand, there are a number of 'in-between' cases – not as fragile as the ones we have studied, not as successful as Botswana or Costa Rica – which represent some hope for the future. Countries such as Rwanda, Liberia or Sierra Leone are currently fortunate to have relatively decent leaders and they have been able to create some improvement, in cooperation with assistance from the outside. We have criticized the idea that Western-style modernization eventually will take place in all countries, but it should be added that fragile states are not doomed to failure, misery and underdevelopment. The 'in-between' cases contain elements which may help spark the virtuous circles of 'success breeds success' that we found in Botswana and Costa Rica. But these elements may also be too weak and thus countervailing forces of 'failure breeds failure' will again come to dominate, as we have seen, for example, in Ivory Coast.

What to Do About Fragile States?

So what, if anything, can be done about fragile states? One major set of suggestions emphasizes the need for more rather than less intervention by outsiders. If intervention is better planned and coordinated, more comprehensive and with a longer time-frame (so the argument goes), there is a good possibility that outsiders can go about 'fixing failed states' (Ghani and Lockhart, 2008). We have already indicated our severe doubts about this proposition. Substantial outside involvement has not led to great results in any of the cases we have examined. In fact, in our success cases there was very little outside involvement at all. Even under more forthcoming conditions, there are serious problems. Take the case of Uganda, a recent darling of the donor community. Given the intense international involvement there over the past decade, one would think there would be a stronger, more effective and more democratic and responsive state. Not the case, argues a recent analysis.

> Measured in terms of state activities, or its extraction capacity, the Ugandan state is still far behind the level it had achieved in the late 1960s. The Ugandan state resembles a patchwork quilt much more than it does a unitary actor. It is deeply embedded in a conflictive network of agencies that are sometimes at odds and sometimes in line with the idea of unitary statehood. The state is not only dependent; it is

> suspended between international agents and local actors and
> their practices and expectations. (Schlichte, 2008: 380)

In other words, external involvement by all kinds of outsiders has led to a new situation of external domination in Uganda. The state has not established control over the security sector. State elites fear the strength of a large and effective military apparatus and thus have allowed a privatization of the means of violence, leaving security to a host of local and international actors. Nor does the state have any effective control over its financial situation. The wealthy bribe their way out of taxation and the political elite are taxed only lightly to avoid disrupting a delicate political balance. Funds from external sources cover most of public investment (Schlichte, 2008: 379). As in colonial times, the state again turns outward. For incumbents (and their allied elites), the relationship with Western or other strong governments is more important than that with anyone else, including local citizens. In sum, this is not a great recipe for escaping fragile statehood.

Our propositions for improvement, therefore, move in another direction. We offer two general proposals: (a) re-examine external conditions and forms of engagement that foster or support the mitigation of fragile statehood; and (b) be ready to do more, and with much greater speed, in emergency situations. Re-examining the role of external conditions and forms of engagement includes a critical look at development cooperation. This is not a new idea, of course. Already in the 1970s, development economist Peter Bauer (1972) described aid as 'a tax on poor people in rich countries that benefits rich people in poor countries' (cited by Moyo, 2009: 67). Towards the end of his life, Gunnar Myrdal (1984) turned against development aid, suggesting that the resources were better spent on relief operations. More recently, William Easterly (2006) has aroused much attention with his critique of aid. In a book provocatively titled *Dead Aid* (2009), Dambisa Moyo argues against traditional development aid to Africa (Moyo 2009). Along the same line, renowned development theorist Goran Hyden (2010) has recently suggested putting development aid to an end, in order to terminate 'the harmful dependency [of African countries] on aid and donors'.

The arguments against the current forms of aid are simple: it creates a culture of dependency that quells local initiative; it orients the middle class towards state funds instead of independent initiatives; it animates widespread corruption in the state apparatus and at all levels of society; it stifles economic growth in recipient countries while donor economies pursue their own benefits; and it diverts the government's attention away from its own people because the government's focus becomes how to extract resources from donors. The extraordinarily high level of aid to fragile states was noted in chapter 2. Africa has received more than $1 trillion in aid over the last sixty years and much of this aid, despite some good intentions of the donors, rather than creating development, has contributed to fragility.

The 'development industry' is well aware of its shortcomings. There are serious attempts to make aid more effective (OECD, 2005); yet the results of such efforts remain to be seen. These new reform efforts may even be stifled by the increasing presence of emerging countries like China, India or Brazil as sources of funds and know-how because these countries attach fewer overt political, humanitarian or ecological conditions for their cooperation. So more emphasis should be laid on helping to create, both internally and externally, the political and economic space needed for effective self-help and for more productive state–society relations. This is, of course on the agenda of the development industry in the context of the current debate on aid effectiveness. But it still is not clear whether this new debate really makes aid in fragile states more effective or simply adds up to another attempt at symbolic problem solving which compensates for a lack of progress on the ground by more progress in conceptual thinking. It has yet to be established what 'empowerment' and 'ownership' mean for fragile states and how they can be put into practice in a stringent way.

Our first proposition – that we re-examine external conditions conducive to the mitigation of fragile statehood – requires rich countries to focus on the international economic and political conditions that define the larger development context for fragile states. There are many aspects of this, including trade relations, market access, investment rules, financial regulation, the rules and regulations of the international organizations, and 'transnational bads', such as smuggling, the drugs trade, the arms trade, international terrorism, and so on. These all constitute the framework conditions within which fragile states function. Our argument is that these framework conditions could be much improved if they are viewed from the perspective of fragile states that want to develop. Since the rich countries control the framework, any substantial change is basically up to them.

It is impossible to cover all the different aspects of international framework conditions here. We comment on two facets of the economic framework and on one major element of 'transnational bads', the trade in small arms. A World Bank research paper asked whether global trade distortions still harm developing country farmers (Anderson and Valenzuela 2006). The starting point is that developing country farmers contribute less than 3 per cent of global GDP, while they account for 43 per cent of global employment and 64 per cent of global agricultural value added. In other words, raising net farmer income is a key element in reducing global poverty. Is the reduction of trade policy distortions, including agricultural subsidies in high-income countries, of importance here?

The answer is a clear 'yes'; poor country market shares and shares of value added would rise markedly if distortions were fully removed, and thus would raise net farmer income.

Unfortunately, rich countries narrow down development options in poor countries in other ways as well. While their own paths to economic strength went through periods of using mercantilist principles of infant-industry protection, they now impose neoliberal principles on poor countries, which amounts to 'kicking away the ladder' for latecomers because national development strategies are constrained (Wade, 2003). In sum, both in industry and in agriculture, rich countries maintain international framework conditions in fragile countries that impede economic growth. That has to change. The international community has to transform its role vis-à-vis fragile states from upholding fragile statehood to providing for the material conditions that would help to overcome it. An example of positive action may be seen in the decision of the European Union to change the rules of origin in its trade relations with its Arab neighbours on the Mediterranean in favour of North African partners. This initiative came in the wake of the 2011 uprising in the respective countries and may help to strengthen trade relations among them, thus improving the external economic framework conditions of social and political change within the region.

Both the licit and illicit trade in arms continues to negatively impact fragile states. The licit trade, including military assistance provided by donor countries, is substantial, particularly when measured as a percentage of fragile states' imports or gross domestic product. The weapons are provided to enable governing elites to outgun their domestic opponents. Their opponents most often obtain their weapons via the illicit trade in small arms, by capturing large caches of weapons or by corrupting or 'turning' military officials who believe the rebels are the more likely winners in the violent struggle. The illicit

trade, which is primarily in small arms such as AK-47s, ena-
bles poorly trained and poorly controlled soldiers to easily kill
and threaten. The small arms proliferation often leads both to
criminal activities which undermine the authority of the government and to political challenges that threaten populations
and governments (Stohl and Grillot, 2009).

While there is relatively little the international community
may do about the vast sea of arms already in circulation, it
may take steps to avoid exacerbating future situations. First, it
would be useful to create greater controls for arms captured or
obtained as a function of interventions and ceasefires and to
prevent their recirculation in the aftermath. Second, it is to be
hoped that the proposed Arms Trade Treaty within the United
Nations will contain measures that will enhance state restraint
in transferring arms to countries with socio-economic and
development challenges, and ensure that these weapons will
not be used to exacerbate conflict and armed violence. As we
have indicated above, the problem here is that it is the great
powers that are home to the world's leading producers and
traders of weapons and there are strong financial incentives
to continue the sale of arms. However, these arms-producing
states must develop strong end-use controls to establish the
destination and user of the weapons and be held accountable
for their enforcement. The international community must
ensure that these arms are not diverted into the illegal market
or transferred to self-interested and irresponsible groups in
third countries.

Studies of economic growth indicate that the higher the
percentage of government expenditures on arms, the lower
the economic growth rate (Singh, 2008). Further, as Robert
Muggah and Peter Batchelor (2003) have convincingly argued,
the pernicious effects on fragile (and other developing) states
also include increases in criminal violence perpetrated with
arms stolen from or sold by the security forces, and thus a

decline in both governmental capacity to protect populations and social trust; the collapse of health and education services, and consistent damage to the social structure; and, ironically, the frequent withdrawal of development assistance because aid workers are threatened by the spiral of violence that easier access to weapons creates. These weapons also provide a much more dangerous environment in the context of emergency situations.

Our second proposition concerns these emergency situations. They can be cases of severe violent conflict that threaten the lives of thousands, sometimes even hundreds of thousands, of civilians; they can also be cases of famine or natural disaster. In these situations, international society should be ready to act with much greater speed and efficiency. The UN World Summit in 2005 did confirm a 'responsibility to protect' – that is, to act when populations are suffering serious harm in conflict; but the meeting also emphasized that this was primarily the responsibility of each individual state, while the international community should merely encourage and help states to exercise this responsibility. Only in the case when a government is manifestly unwilling or unable to protect its people from war crimes, genocide, ethnic cleansing and crimes against humanity may international society represented through the Security Council intervene, if necessary by force. However, the Security Council itself is not always willing or able to act (Jentleson, 2007: 285). As each disaster case unfolds, a process of painful and slow negotiations occurs because of unclear spheres of responsibility. Thus interventions continue to remain highly selective and hesitant, even in cases of serious humanitarian concern.

International society has no autonomous capacity in this regard; it relies on the willingness of member states to do something. In other words, with little willingness among those great powers that have the capacity for intervention, nothing much is done. The reluctance to act in a coherent way, on the one hand, reflects the complexities of intervention mentioned above (chapter 4); on the other, it affirms the fact that states will only help others when this also helps them. The UN Charter calls for the peaceful settlement of disputes and for collective action, including the use of force if peace cannot be maintained or restored otherwise. From early on, peacekeeping was invented to extend the scope of possible action. Since the end of the Cold War, this tool has been further developed to include an active role of peacekeeping forces in upholding peace agreements against so-called 'spoilers'. At the same time, peace missions have become ever more encompassing. This development confirms our observation that any kind of intervention develops a dynamic of its own that is difficult to control. Yet the professionalization of peace missions is probably the most promising international instrument for dealing with domestic conflict in fragile states. As part of this professionalization, external actors have to be provided with adequate information on the political and cultural environment in which they are to act. This goes especially for fragile states in which the state is not a settled bureaucracy but manifests itself more in the continuous negotiation of authority in a context of potentially violent self-help. For instance, with regard to the DRC, it has been argued that in order to assure a positive impact of the largest UN Peace Mission (MONUC), two innovations are required: a greater focus on trans-border players and dynamics and 'a shift from ad hoc humanitarian approaches to a more comprehensive effort that addresses trade-offs inherent in the regional war economy' (Gilpin and Funai, 2009: 1). Along the same line, Séverine Autesserre (2009) calls for a closer look at local agendas that shape the fighting in the north-eastern provinces. This would complicate the issue, but it seems that any form of intervention that does not pay heed to these complications is doomed to fail anyhow.

In addition, international society ought to think about more innovative moves. Various proposals merit investigation, such as decertifying governments that inflict serious harm on their populations; 'smart sanctions' (Cortwright and Lopez, 2002) that target the perpetrators; and financial sanctions that deny global access for corrupt regimes and predatory elites.

As already mentioned, according to the 'responsibility to protect' in its official 2005 version, the primary responsibility for the protection of people in conflict lies with the respective governments. The international community is to assist these governments in living up to their responsibility or to intervene if necessary. Beyond such assistance and intervention, the international community can make sure that the external framework conditions point in the right direction. This is to say that the 'responsibility to protect', if taken seriously, would call for a stronger regard for humanitarian considerations in any debate on the rules by which the world economy functions.

Even under the best of conditions, the mitigation of fragile statehood by outsiders will be difficult to achieve. Thus, while we believe that the international community should exercise great caution before interfering with fragile statehood, it must not be complacent with regard to the suffering of people. Balancing the need for caution with due consideration of the costs and benefits of both action and inaction in times of crisis as well as in the longer term will continue to be at the heart of the international community's fragile state dilemma.

References

Acemoglu, D., Johnson, S. and Robinson, J. (2003). 'An African Success Story: Botswana', in Dani Rodrik (ed.), *In Search of Prosperity: Analytical Narrative on Economic Growth*. Princeton: Princeton University Press, pp. 80–119.

Adler, E. and Barnett, M. (1998). *Security Communities*. Cambridge: Cambridge University Press.

Ameringer, C. D. (1982). *Democracy in Costa Rica*. New York: Praeger.

Anderson, B. (1991). *Imagined Communities: Reflections on the Origin and Spread of Nationalism*. London: Verso.

Anderson, K. and Valenzuela, E. (2006). Do Global Trade Distortions Still Harm Developing Country Farmers? Accessed 15 July 2011 at *http://siteresources.worldbank.org/INTTRADERESEARCH/Resources/544824-1146153362267/AgVADis.pdf*

Anderson, M. (1999). *Do No Harm: How Aid Can Support Peace – or War*. Boulder, CO: Lynne Rienner Publishers.

Anderson, P. (1974). *Lineages of the Absolutist State*. London: New Left Books.

Autesserre, S. (2009). 'Hobbes and the Congo: Frames, Local Violence, and International Intervention', *International Organization*, 63:2, 249–80.

Barfield, T. (2010). *Afghanistan: A Cultural and Political History*. Princeton: Princeton University Press.

Bauer, P. (1972). *Dissent on Development*. Cambridge, MA: Harvard University Press.

Baylis, J. (1999). 'European Security between the "Logic of Anarchy" and the "Logic of Community", in Carl C. Hodge (ed.), *Redefining European Security*. London: Garland Publishing, pp. 13–28.

Bellamy, A. (2004). 'Ethics and Intervention: The "Humanitarian Exception" and the Problem of Abuse in the Case of Iraq', *Journal of Peace Research*, 41:2, 131–47.

Bercovitch, J. and Jackson, R. (2009). *Conflict Resolution in the Twenty-First Century: Principles, Methods, and Approaches.* Ann Arbor, University of Michigan Press.

Berdal, M. and Malone, D. (eds) (2000). *Greed and Grievance: Economic Agendas in Civil War.* Boulder, CO: Lynne Rienner Publishers.

Berman, H. J. (1993). *Faith and Order: The Reconciliation of Law and Religion.* Atlanta, GA: Scholars Press.

Beulier, S. (2003). 'Explaining Botswana's Success: The Critical Role of Post-Colonial Policy', *Cato Journal*, 232, 227–40.

Bothe, M., O'Connell, M. E. and Ronzitti, N. (eds) (2004). *Redefining Sovereignty: The Use of Force after the End of the Cold War: New Options, Lawful and Legitimate?* Ardsley, NY: Transnational Publishers .

Braathen, E., Bøås, M. and Saether, G. (2000). 'Ethnicity Kills? Social Struggles for Power, Resources and Identities in the Neo-Patrimonial State', in E. Braathen, M. Bøås and G. Saether (eds), *Ethnicity Kills? The Politics of War, Peace and Ethnicity in Sub-Saharan Africa.* Basingstoke: Macmillan, pp. 3–22.

Brahimi, L. and Pickering, T. (2011). 'Settling the Afghan War', *The New York Times*, 23 March. Accessed 20 July 2011 at *http://www. nytimes.com/2011/03/23/opinion/23brahimi.html*

Brock, L. (2009). 'Protecting People in Conflict: Responsibility or Threat?', in M. Brzoska and A. Krohn (eds), *Overcoming Armed Violence in a Complex World.* Opladen and Farmington Hills, MI: Budrich UniPress, pp. 223–42.

Brown, M. E. (1997). 'The Causes of Internal Conflict', in M. E. Brown (ed.), *Nationalism and Ethnic Conflict.* Cambridge, MA: MIT Press, pp. 1–31.

Brunnee, J. and Toope, S. (2004). 'Slouching towards New Just Wars: The Hegemon after September 11th', *International Relations*, 18:4, 405–23.

Buzan, B. (1991). *People, States, and Fear*, 2nd edn. New York: Harvester Wheatsheaf.

Byman, D. L. and Waxman, M. C. (2000). 'Kosovo and the Great Air Power Debate', *International Security*, 24:4, 5–38.

Cahill, D. (2007). 'Donor Engagement in Fragile States: A Case Study of Donors in the DRC and the OECD Principles for Good International Engagement in Fragile States', Background Paper. Antwerp: International Peace Information Service/Fatal Transactions.

Call, C. T. (2008). 'The Fallacy of the "Failed State"', *Third World Quarterly*, 29:8, 1491–507.

Callaghy, T. (1991). 'Africa and the World Economy: Caught between a Rock and a Hard Place', in J. Harbeson and D. Rotschild (eds), *Africa in World Politics*. Boulder, CO: Westview, pp. 39–69.

Cardoso, C. (1991). 'The Liberal Era', in L. Bethell (ed.), *Central America since Independence*. Cambridge: Cambridge University Press, pp. 37–68.

Carothers, T. (2002). 'The End of the Transitions Paradigm', *Journal of Democracy*, 13:1, 5–21.

Carroll, T. and Carroll, B. (2004). 'The Rapid Emergence of Civil Society in Botswana', *Commonwealth and Comparative Politics*, 42:3, 333–55.

Carter, A. B. and Perry. W. (1999). *Preventive Defense: A New Strategy for America*. Washington, DC: Brookings.

Chandler, D. (2006). 'Back to the Future: The Limits of Neo-Wilsonian Ideals of Exporting Democracy', *Review of International Studies*, 32:3, 475–94.

Clapham, C. (1993). 'The *Longue Durée* of the African State', *African Affairs*, 93, 433–9.

Clapham, C. (1996). 'Rwanda: The Perils of Peace-Making', paper for African Studies Biennal Conference, University of Bristol.

Clapham, C. (2003). 'The Challenge of the State in a Globalized World', in J. Milliken (ed.), *State Failure, Collapse and Reconstruction*. Oxford: Blackwell, pp. 25–44.

Collier, P. (2007). *The Bottom Billion: Why the Poorest Countries Are Failing and What Can Be Done about It*. Oxford: Oxford University Press.

Collier, P. and Hoeffler, A. (2001). *Greed and Grievance in Civil War*. Washington, DC: World Bank.

Copson, R. (2001). 'Africa: U.S. Foreign Assistance Issues'. Congressional Research Service Brief, Washington, DC.

Coquery-Vidrovitch, C. (1976). 'The Political Economy of the African Peasantry and Modes of Production', in P. Gutkind and I. Wallerstein (eds), *The Political Economy of Contemporary Africa*. Beverly Hills: Sage Publications, pp. 90–111.

Cortwright, D. and Lopez, G. A. (eds) (2002). *Smart Sanctions: Targeting Economic Statecraft*. Plymouth: Rowman and Littlefield.

Cruz, C. (2005). *Political Culture and Institutional Development in Costa Rica and Nicaragua*. Cambridge: Cambridge University Press.

Darwin, J. (2007). *After Tamerlane: The Global History of Empire*. London: Allen Lane.

Davis, H. P. (1928). *Black Democracy: The Story of Haiti*. New York: The Dial Press.

Deibert, M. (2009). 'Challenges to Haiti's Security Gains'. Talk presented to the Applied Research Center and the Latin American and Caribbean Center at Florida International University in Miami, Florida, August 2009. Reprinted at Alterpresse.org, 10 October 2009. Accessed 20 July 2011 at *http://www.alterpresse.org/spip.php?article8867*

Deutsch, K. W., Burrell, S. W., Kann, R. W., Lee, M. Jr, Lichterman, M., Lindgren, R. E., Loewenheim, F. L. and van Wagenen, R. W. (1957). *Political Community and the North Atlantic Area*. Princeton: Princeton University Press.

Dewitt, D., Haglund, D. and Kriton, J. (eds) (1993). *Building a New Global Order*. Oxford: Oxford University Press.

di John, J. (2010). 'The Concept, Causes and Consequences of Failed States: A Critical Review of the Literature and Agenda for Research with Specific Reference to Sub-Saharan Africa', *European Journal of Development Research*, 22:1, 10–30.

Dijkzeul, D. (2008). 'Towards a Framework of the Study of "No War, No Peace" Societies'. Working Paper 2. Bern: Swisspeace.

Duffield, M. (2001). *Global Governance and New Wars: The Merging of Development and Security*. London: Zed Books.

Easterly, W. (2006). *The White Man's Burden: Why the West's Efforts to Aid the World Have Done So Much Ill and So Little Good*. New York: Penguin Press.

Economist Intelligence Unit (2008). *Costa Rica, Country Profile 2008*. London, The Economist.

Engberg-Petersen, L., Andersen, L. and Stepputat, F. (2008). 'Fragile Situations: Current Debates and Central Dilemmas'. Paper. Copenhagen: Danish Institute for International Studies.

Englebert, P. (2003). Why Congo Persists: Sovereignty, Globalization and the Violent Reproduction of a Weak State. QEH Working Paper No. 95. Oxford University: Queen Elizabeth House.

Englebert, P. (2009). *Africa: Unity, Sovereignty, and Sorrow*. Boulder, CO: Lynne Rienner Publishers.

Evans, P., Rueschemeyer, D. and Skocpol, T. (eds) (1985). *Bringing the State Back In*. Cambridge: Cambridge University Press.

Farer, T. J. (2003). 'Humanitarian Intervention before and after 9/11', in J. L. Holzgrefe and Robert O. Keohane (eds), *Humanitarian Intervention: Ethical, Legal and Political Dilemmas*. New York: Cambridge University Press, pp. 53–90.

Fatton, R., Jr (2002). *Haiti's Predatory Republic: The Unending Transition to Democracy*. Boulder, CO: Lynne Rienner Publishers.

Fearon, J. and Laitin, D. (2000) 'Violence and the Social Construction of Ethnic Identity', *International Organization*, 54:4, 845–77.

Fearon, J. and Laitin, D. (2003). 'Ethnicity, Insurgency, and Civil War', *American Political Science Review*, 97:1, 75–95.

Fukuyama, F. (1992). *The End of History and the Last Man*. New York: Avon.

Fukuyama, F. (2004). 'The Imperative of State-Building', *Journal of Democracy*, 15:2, 17–31.

Gaddis J. L. (1999). 'Living in Candlestick Park', *Atlantic Monthly*, April, 65–74. Accessed 15 July 2011 at *http://www.theatlantic.com/past/docs/issues/99apr/9904candlestick.htm*

Geis, A., Brock, L. and Müller, H. (2006). *Democratic Wars: Looking at the Dark Side of Democratic Peace*. Basingstoke: Macmillan.

Ghani, A. and Lockhart, C. (2008). *Fixing Failed States: A Framework for Rebuilding a Fractured World*. New York: Oxford University Press.

Gilpin, M. C. and Funai, G. (2009). 'Beyond Emergency Responses in the Democratic Republic of Congo: Regional Solutions for a Regional Conflict'. USIPEACE Briefing. Washington, DC: United States Institute of Peace.

Giustozzi, A. (2009). *Empires of Mud. War and Warlords in Afghanistan*. London: Hurst.

Goldstone, J. A. (2009). 'Pathways to State Failure', in H. Starr (ed.), *Dealing with Failed States*. London: Routledge, pp. 5–17.

Good, K. (1992). 'Interpreting the Exceptionality of Botswana', *Journal of African Studies*, 30:1, 69–95.

Good, K. (2008). *Diamonds, Dispossession and Democracy in Botswana*. London: James Currey.

Hagmann, T. (2007). 'Bringing the Sultan Back in: Elders as Traditional Peacemakers in Ethiopia's Somalia Region', in L. Buur and H. M. Kyed (eds), *State Recognition and Democratization in Sub-Sahara Africa*. New York: Palgrave, pp. 31–51.

Hagmann, T. and Hoehne, M. (2009). 'Failures of the State Failure Debate: Evidence from the Somali Territories', *Journal of International Development*, 21, 42–57.

Hagmann, T. and Péclard, D. (2010). 'Negotiating Statehood: Dynamics of Power and Domination in Africa', *Development and Change*, 41:4, 539–62.

Haiti Innovation (2010). Ban Ki-moon address to the Haiti donors' conference, 31 March. Accessed 20 July 2011 at *http://www.haitiinnovation.org/en/2010/04/02/2010-haiti-donors-conference-and-way-ahead*

Harbom, L. and Wallensteen, P. (2009). 'Armed Conflicts 1946–2008', *Journal of Peace Research*, 46:4, 577–87.

Hartung, W. (2001). 'The New Business of War', *Ethics & International Affairs*, 15:1, 79–96.

Haskin, G. (2005). *The Tragic State of the Congo*. New York: Algora Publishing.

Hayter, T. (1971). *Aid as Imperialism*. Harmondsworth: Penguin.

Herbst, J. (2000). *States and Power in Africa: Comparative Lessons in Authority and Control*. Princeton: Princeton University Press.

Herz, J. (1950). 'Idealist Internationalism and the Security Dilemma', *World Politics*, 2:2, 157–80.

Hobbes, T. (1960). *Leviathan* (with an introduction by M. Oakeshott). Oxford: Basil Blackwell.

Hodge, C. (1999). 'Germany: Is Sound Diplomacy the Better Part of Security?', in C. Hodge (ed.), *Redefining European Security*. London: Garland Publishing, pp. 181–207.

Howe, H. (2001). *Ambiguous Order: Military Forces in African States*. Boulder, CO: Lynne Rienner Publishers.

Human Security Report (2005). *Human Security Report: War and Peace in the 21st Century*. Accessed 20 July 2011 at *http://www.hsrgroup.org/human-security-reports/2005/overview.aspx*

Huntington, S. P. (1992). *The Third Wave: Democratization in the Late Twentieth Century*. Norman: University of Oklahoma Press.

Hyden, G. (1980). *Beyond Ujamaa in Tanzania: Underdevelopment and an Uncaptured Peasantry*. Berkeley: University of California Press.

Hyden, G. (2010). 'Rethinking Development in Africa'. Accessed 15 July 2011 at *http://www.nai.uu.se/forum/entries/2010/08/25/rethinking-development-in/index.xml*

Jackson, R. (1990). *Quasi-States: Sovereignty, International Relations and the Third World*. Cambridge: Cambridge University Press.

Jackson, R. (1992). 'Juridical Statehood in Sub-Saharan Africa', *Journal of International Affairs*, 46:1, 1–16.

Jackson, R. (1995). 'International Community beyond the Cold War', in G. M. Lyons and M. Mastanduno (eds), *Beyond Westphalia? State Sovereignty and International Intervention*. Baltimore: Johns Hopkins University Press, pp. 59–87.

Jackson, R. and Rosberg, C. (1982). 'Why Weak States Persist: The Empirical and the Juridical in Statehood', *World Politics*, 35:1, 1–24.

Jackson, R. and Rosberg, C. (1994). 'The Political Economy of African Personal Rule', in D. E. Apter and C. G. Rosberg (eds), *Political Development and the New Realism in Sub-Saharan Africa*. Charlottesville: University Press of Virginia, 291–325.

Jenkins, K. and Plowden, W. (2006). *Governance and Nationbuilding: The Failure of International Intervention*. Cheltenham: Edward Elgar.

Jentleson, B. (2007). 'Yet Again: Humanitarian Intervention and the Challenges of "Never Again"', in J. Crocker, F. O. Hamson and P. Aall (eds.), *Leashing the Dogs of War: Conflict Management in a Divided World*. Washington, DC: Institute of Peace, pp. 277–97.

Job, B. (ed.) (1992). *The Insecurity Dilemma: National Security of Third World States*. Boulder, CO: Lynne Rienner Publishers.

Jones, B. G. (2005). '"Failed States": An Ideology of the Imperialism of Our Time'. Paper for World International Studies Committee Conference, Istanbul, Turkey, 24–7 August.

Jung, D. (ed.) (2003). *Shadow Globalization, Ethnic Conflicts and New Wars: A Political Economy of Intra-State War*. London: Routledge.

Kagan, R. (2007). 'Return of History', *Policy Review*, 144, 1–17.

Kaldor, M. (1999). *New and Old Wars: Organized Violence in a Global Era*. Cambridge: Polity.

Kalyvas, S. (2006). *The Logic of Violence in Civil War*. New York: Cambridge University Press.

Kaplan, Robert D. (1994). 'The Coming Anarchy', *Atlantic Monthly*, 273:2, 44–76.

Keen, D. (2000). 'Incentives and Disincentives for Violence', in M. Berdal and D. Malone (eds), *Greed and Grievance: Economic Agendas in Civil Wars*. Boulder, CO: Lynne Rienner Publishers, pp. 19–41.

Keohane, R. O. (1995). 'Hobbes's Dilemma and Institutional Change in World Politics: Sovereignty in International Society', in H.-H. Holm and G. Sørensen (eds), *Whose World Order? Uneven Globalization and the End of the Cold War*. Boulder, CO: Westview, pp. 165–87.

Kessel, J. (1968). *The Horsemen*. New York: Littlehampton Book Services.

Kingston-Mann, E. (1999). *In Search of the True West: Culture, Economics and Problems of Russian Development*, Princeton: Princeton University Press.

Knight, A. and Yamashita, M. (1993). 'The United Nations' Contribution to International Peace and Security', in D. David,

D. Haglund and J. Kriton (eds), *Building a New Global Order*. Oxford: Oxford University Press, pp. 284–312.

Knudsen, T. B. (1999). Humanitarian Intervention and International Society. Ph.D. thesis. Aarhus University, Department of Political Science.

Krasner, S. (2009). 'Sharing Sovereignty: New Institutions for Collapsed and Failing States', in S. Krasner, *Power, the State and Sovereignty: Essays on International Relations*. London: Routledge, pp. 232–53.

Kreuzer, P. (2009). 'Philippine Governance: Merging Politics and Crime'. PRIF Report No. 93. Frankfurt/M.: Peace Research Institute Frankfurt.

Lange, M. (2009). *Lineages of Despotism and Development: British Colonialism and State Power*. Chicago: University of Chicago Press.

MacFarlane, N., Thielking, C. and Weiss, T. (2004). 'The Responsibility to Protect: Is Anyone Interested in Humanitarian Intervention?', *Third World Quarterly – Journal of Emerging Areas*, 25:5, 977–92.

McGowan, P. (2003). 'African Military Coups d'État, 1956–2001: Frequency, Trends and Distribution', *The Journal of Modern African Studies*, 41:3, 339–70.

Maingot, A. P. (1996). 'Sovereign Consensus versus State-Centric Sovereignty', in T. Farer (ed.), *Beyond Sovereignty. Collectively Defending Democracy in the Americas*. Baltimore/London: Johns Hopkins University Press, pp. 189–205.

Mann, M. (1984). 'The Autonomous Power of the State: Its Origins, Mechanisms, and Results', *Archives Européenes de Sociologie*, 5, 185–213.

Meredith, M. (2006). *The State of Africa: A History of Fifty Years of Independence*, London: The Free Press.

Meyer, J. W., Boli, J., Thomas, G. M. and Ramirez, F. O. (1997). 'World Society and the Nation-State', *American Journal of Sociology*, 103, 144–81.

Migdal, J. S. (1988). *Strong Societies and Weak States: State–Society Relations and State Capabilities in the Third World*. Princeton: Princeton University Press.

Migdal, J. S. (1994). 'The State in Society: An Approach to Struggles for Domination', in J. S. Migdal, A. Kohli and V. Shue (eds), *State Power and Social Forces: Domination and Transformation in the Third World*. Cambridge: Cambridge University Press, pp. 7–34.

Migdal, J. S. (2001). *State in Society: Studying How States and Societies*

Transform and Constitute Each Other. Cambridge: Cambridge University Press.

Miller, J. D. B. (1981). *The World of States: Connected Essays*. New York: St Martin's Press.

Moyo, D. (2009). *Dead Aid: Why Aid Is Not Working and How There Is Another Way for Africa*. London: Allen Lane.

Muggah, R. and Batchelor, P. (2002). 'Development Held Hostage: Assessing the Effects of Small Arms on Human Development'. United Nations Development Programme. Accessed 15 July 2011 at *http://www.gsdrc.org/go/display/document/legacyid/466*

Myrdal, G. (1984). 'International Inequality and Foreign Aid in Retrospect', in G. M. Meier and D. Seers (eds), *Pioneers in Development*. Washington, DC: World Bank; Oxford: Oxford University Press, pp. 149–65.

Norton-Taylor, R. (2011). 'Britain Has Allowed Its Weapons to be Used for Internal Repression, MPs Say', *Guardian*, 5 April. Accessed 15 July 2011 at *http://www.guardian.co.uk/world/2011/apr/05/britain-let-weapons-be-used-for-repression*

NSS (2002). *The National Security Strategy of the United States of America*. Washington, DC: The White House, Office of the President of the United States.

OECD (2005). *The Paris Declaration on Aid Effectiveness and the Accra Agenda for Action*. Accessed 20 July 2011 at *http://www.oecd.org/dataoecd/11/41/34428351.pdf*

OECD (2007). 'Principles for Good International Engagement in Fragile States & Situations'. Development Assistance Committee, April. Paris: Organization for Economic Co-operation and Development. Accessed 15 July 2011 at *http://www.oecd.org/dataoecd/61/45/38368714.pdf*

Packenham, T. (1992). *The Scramble for Africa: The White Man's Conquest of the Dark Continent from 1876–1912*. New York: Avon.

Palmer, S. and Molina, I. (2004). *The Costa Rica Reader*. Durham, NC: Duke University Press.

Partlow, J. (2009). 'Al Qaeda Declines, Taliban Rise in Afghanistan', *San Francisco Chronicle*, 11 November.

Peeler, J. A. (1985). *Latin American Democracies: Colombia, Costa Rica, Venezuela*. Chapel Hill, NC: University of North Carolina Press.

Pitcher, A., Moran, M. and Johnston, M. (2009). 'Rethinking Patrimonialism and Neopatrimonialism in Africa', *African Studies Review*, 52:1, 125–56.

Prunier, G. (1995). *The Rwanda Crisis*. New York: Columbia University Press.

Prunier, G. (2009). *From Genocide to Continental War: The 'Congolese' Conflict and the Crisis of Contemporary Africa*. London: Hurst.

Rashid, A. (2001). *Taliban: Islam, Oil and the New Great Game in Central Asia*. New Haven: Yale Notabene Books.

Record, J. (2002). 'Collapsed Countries, Casualty Dread, and the New American Way of War', *Parameters*, Summer, 32, 4–23.

Reno, W. (2006). 'Congo: From State Collapse to "Absolutism", to State Failure', *Third World Quarterly*, 27:1, 43–56.

Rice, S. E. (2003). 'The New National Security Strategy: Focus on Failed States Policy'. Policy Brief no. 116. Washington, DC: Brookings Institution.

Rice, S. E. and Patrick, S. (2008). *Index of State Weakness in the Developing World*. Washington, DC: Brookings Institution.

Roberts, A. (2000). 'NATO's Humanitarian War over Kosovo', *Survival*, 41:3, 102–3.

Roberts, M. (2010). 'The Implications of MONUC's Withdrawal on Child Soldiering in the DRC'. Institute for Security Studies (ISS). Accessed 15 July 2011 at *http://www.reliefweb.int/rw/rwb.nsf/db900sid/EGUA-868S6N?OpenDocument*

Robinson, J. (2008). 'The Latin American Equilibrium', in F. Fukuyama (ed.), *Falling Behind: Explaining the Development Gap between Latin America and the United States*. Oxford: Oxford University Press, pp. 161–93.

Rosecrance, R. (1986). *The Rise of the Trading State: Commerce and Conquest in the Modern World*. New York: Basic Books.

Rosecrance, R. (1999). *The Rise of the Virtual State*. New York: Basic Books.

Sachs, J. (2006). 'How Aid Can Work', *New York Review of Books*, 21 December. Accessed 15 July 2011 at *http://www.nybooks.com/articles/archives/2006/dec/21/how-aid-can-work/*

Saideman, S. M., Lanoue, D. J., Campenni M. and Stanton, S. (2002). 'Democratization, Political Institutions, and Ethnic Conflict: A Pooled Time-Series Analysis, 1985–1998', *Comparative Political Studies*, 35:1, 103–29.

Saikal, A. (2005). 'Afghanistan's Weak State and Strong Society', in S. Chesterman, M. Ignatieff and R. Thakur (eds), *Making States Work: State Failure and the Crisis of Governance*. New York: United Nations University Press, pp. 193–209.

Schlichte, K. (2008). 'Uganda or: The Internationalization of Rule', *Civil Wars*, 10:4, 369–83.

Schmeidl, S. (2009). '"Prêt-a-Porter States": How the McDonaldization of State-Building Misses the Mark in Afghanistan', in *Building Peace in the Absence of States: Challenging the Discourse on State Failure*. Berghof Handbook Dialogue Series No. 8. Berlin: Berghof Research Center, pp. 67–78. Accessed 15 July 2011 at *http://www.berghof-handbook.net/documents/publications/dialogue8_schmeidl_karokhail_comm.pdf*

Seligson, M. A. (1980). *Peasants of Costa Rica and the Development of Agrarian Capitalism*. Madison: University of Wisconsin Press.

Shafer, D. M. (1994). *Winners and Losers: How Sectors Shape the Developmental Prospects of States*. Ithaca, NY: Cornell University Press.

Shah, K. (2009). 'The Failure of State Building and the Promise of State Failure: Reinterpreting the Security–Development Nexus in Haiti', *Third World Quarterly*, 30:1, 17–34.

Singer, P. (2005). 'Outsourcing War', *Foreign Affairs*, 84:2, 119–32.

Singh, A. (2008). 'Socio-Economic Impact of Arms Transfers to Developing Countries', *Peace & Conflict Review*, 2:1. Accessed 15 July 2011 at *http://www.review.upeace.org/pdf.cfm?articulo=75&ejemplar=14*

Somalia-Unosom II (1997). Accessed on 20 July 2011 at *http://www.un.org/Depts/DPKO/Missions/unosomi.htm*

Sørensen, G. (1991). *Democracy, Dictatorship and Development: Economic Development in Selected Regimes of the Third World*. Basingstoke: Macmillan.

Sørensen, G. (1996). 'Development as a Hobbesian Dilemma', *Third World Quarterly*, 17:5, 903–16.

Stohl, C. and Stohl, M. (2007). 'Networks of Terror: Theoretical Assumptions and Pragmatic Consequences', *Communication Theory*, 47:2, 93–124.

Stohl, M. (1987). 'Outside of a Small Circle of Friends: States, Genocide, Mass Killing and the Role of Bystanders', *Journal of Peace Research*, 24:2, 151–66.

Stohl, R. and Grillot, S. (2009). *The International Arms Trade*. Cambridge: Polity.

Thorstensen, L. (2007). Does Ethnicity Matter? MA thesis, Aarhus University, Department of Political Science.

Tillema, H. K. (1989). 'Foreign Overt Military Intervention in the Nuclear Age', *Journal of Peace Research*, 26:2, 179–96.

Tilly, C. (1975). 'Reflections on the History of European State-Making', in C. Tilly (ed.), *The Formation of National States in Western Europe*. Princeton: Princeton University Press, pp. 3–83.

Tilly, C. (1992). *Coercion, Capital, and European States, AD 990–1990*. Oxford: Blackwell.

Trotha, T. von (1997). 'Zur Soziologie der Gewalt Trotha', in T. Von Trotha (ed.), *Soziologie der Gewalt*. Opladen: Westdeutscher Verlag, pp. 9–56.

UN (1994). *Report of the Secretary General on the Situation in Rwanda*, S/1994/640. New York: United Nations.

UN (2000). *United Nations Millennium Declaration*. Accessed 15 July 2011 at *http://www.un.org/millennium/declaration/ares552e.htm*

UN (2002). Interim Report of the Panel of Experts on the Illegal Exploitation of Natural Resources and Other Forms of Wealth of the Democratic Republic of the Congo (22 May). New York: United Nations.

UN (2004). The Secretary General's High-Level Panel on Threats, Challenges and Change, *A More Secure World: Our Shared Responsibility*. Delivered to the General Assembly, U.N. Doc. A/59/565 (2 December). New York: United Nations.

UNDP (2005). *Human Development Report 2005*. New York: Oxford University Press.

UNDP (2009). *Human Development Report 2009*. London: Palgrave.

van de Walle, N. (2004). 'Are Botswana and Mauritius *Sui Generis*?' Unpublished conference paper, 1.9.

Wade, R. H. (2003). 'What Strategies Are Available for Developing Countries Today? The World Trade Organization and the Shrinking of "Development Space"', *Review of International Political Economy*, 10:4, 621–44.

Waldman, M. (2008). 'Falling Short: Aid Effectiveness in Afghanistan'. ACBAR advocacy series, March. Accessed 15 July 2011 at *http://www. eisf.eu/resources/item.asp?d=1587*

Walt, S. M. (2002). 'Beyond Bin Laden: Reshaping US Foreign Policy', *International Security*, 26:3, 56–78.

Weber, M. (1946). *From Max Weber: Essays in Sociology*. New York: Oxford University Press.

Weiss, T. (2004). 'The Sunset of Humanitarian Intervention? The Responsibility to Protect in a Unipolar Era', *Security Dialogue*, 35:2, 135–53.

Weiss, T. (2007). *Humanitarian Intervention: Ideas in Action*. Cambridge: Polity.

Wolff, J. and Wurm, I. (2011). 'Towards a Theory of External Democracy Promotion: A Proposal for Theoretical Classification', *Security Dialogue*, 42:1, 77–96.

World Bank (1994). *Adjustment in Africa: Reforms, Results, and the Road Ahead*. New York: Oxford University Press.

World Bank (2009). *Country Partnership Strategy for the Republic of Botswana 2009–2013*. Washington, DC: World Bank.

Wulf, H. (2005). *Internationalizing and Privatizing War and Peace*. Houndmills: Palgrave.

Young, C. and Turner, T. (1985). *The Rise and Decline of the Zairian State*. Madison: University of Wisconsin Press.

Yousaf, M. and Adkin, M. (1992). *The Bear Trap: Afghanistan's Untold Story*. Barnsley: Pen & Sword Books.

Zacher, M. W. (2001). 'The Territorial Integrity Norm: International Boundaries and the Use of Force', *International Organization*, 55:2, 215–50.

Zinecker, H. (2009). 'Regime Hybridity in Developing Countries: Achievements and Limitations of New Research on Transitions', *International Studies Review*, 11:2, 302–31.

Index